The Several Lives of a Victorian Vet

by

JEAN WARE and HUGH HUNT

St. Martin's Press
New York

If you want glory, you must die
— Old Welsh Proverb

Library of Congress Cataloging in Publication Data

Ware, Jean.
   The several lives of a Victorian vet.

   1.   Evans, Griffith H., 1835-1935.   2.   Veter-
inarians—Great Britain—Biography.   I.   Hunt,
Hugh, joint author.   II.   Title.
SF613.E9W37   636.089′092′4   [B]   80-14674
ISBN 0-312-71332-0

CONTENTS

One	Prelude by Jean Ware – The Centenarian	1
Two	Boyhood in Wild Wales	11
Three	A Student in Victorian London	25
Four	The Vet's Assistant	31
Five	Aboard "The Great Eastern"	42
Six	The Body Snatchers	50
Seven	Colonial Canada	58
Eight	An Interview with Abraham Lincoln	68
Nine	Through the Federal Lines	80
Ten	Religion under the Microscope	92
Eleven	Marriage	100
Twelve	An Army Vet in India	111
Thirteen	Ordeal in Bengal	130
Fourteen	Pioneer on the North West Frontier	153
Fifteen	Banishment	164
Sixteen	The Queen Intervenes	181
Seventeen	A Liberal in the Land of Lloyd George	190
Eighteen	The Long Sunset	199
Index		211

Tŷ Mawr, the 18th century farmhouse, near Towyn, Merioneth, where Griffith Evans was born.

FOREWORD

By John Jones
Professor of Poetry in the University of Oxford

This is a story spanning one hundred years and three continents. It presents the American Civil War at first hand through British eyes, and Victorian India in the aftermath of the Mutiny.

Yet its heart is one of the smallest countries on earth, Wales, and its subject is one man – Griffith Evans, vet, doctor, mystic, feminist, brilliant scientist, vivid diarist and quaintest (but also tenderest) of letter-writers. He was born two years before Queen Victoria came to the throne, and on his hundredth birthday in 1935, he was the last European who had known Abraham Lincoln personally.

Jean Ware and Hugh Hunt have shaped a tale which grips the imagination. I want to call it poetic. I *will* call it poetic! Whereas much that is verse is not poetry, very occasionally I read prose which has the flavour and excitement, the sheer push and punch, the laughter and the tears, I really mean the truth, of poetic narrative. If you suspect a Welsh plot, forget about it. This book, like the best wines, is meant to travel. And it will.

Oxford
2 June 1979

ACKNOWLEDGEMENTS

We have been fortunate that the whole of Dr Evans' hundred years was so well documented thanks to the devotion of his daughter, Dr Erie Evans, who preserved his Canadian and American journals, his letters to his wife from India and hers to him, and other correspondence; took down his reminiscences and stories and copied documents. Our thanks are due to Mr J W Barber-Lomax, MA, MRCVS, BSc, formerly assistant director of the Wellcome Institute for the History of Medicine, who gave unsparingly of his time and advice; to the late Dr R F Montgomerie, FRCVS; to the Keeper of Manuscripts at the National Library of Wales; and to the librarians of the City of Liverpool, the Osler Library at McGill University, Montreal, the Liverpool School of Tropical Medicine, the Royal Veterinary College, London, and the RAVC Museum, Aldershot.

We also thank the many friends and helpers who have kindly answered enquiries.

We have, throughout this book, adopted the spelling of Welsh names according to the usage of the period.

J W
H H

List of Illustrations

Ty Mawr, the 18th century farmhouse near   *Frontispiece*
Towyn, Merioneth, where Griffith Evans was
born.

                                            Between Pages
Jean Ware: "He always called me Sian."   22-23

Brynknyallt, Bangor: Griffith Evans' retirement
home.

Griff receiving a scroll from the Royal
Veterinary College on his hundreth birthday.

Silhouette of Griff aged 14 and his sister Maria.

Griff's father, Evan Evans. "His wish to please
everyone was to bring him to ruin."

Griff as a schoolboy.

Towyn as Griff knew it in the mid-nineteenth
century.

The face of compassion. Griffith Evans at 76   38-39
photographed by his son.

Hundreth birthday telegrams from the King and
Queen, the Prince of Wales and Lloyd George. Ll
G wrote ' "felicitations" but the Post Office
transmitted it as "solicitations" .'

At the age of 36, Griffith Evans, newly married,   70-71
was looking "much better fed".

"The Great Eastern" in which Griff sailed to
Canada in charge of more than 100 horses. "The
most wonderful ship ever built."

Abraham Lincoln.

General Meade.

General Butler.

A pass issued to Lieutenant Evans during his
tour of the American Civil War battlefields.

Katie aged 45 — "her gossipy tea parties became   86-87
a legend".

Between Pages

Griff's sister Eliza: "She must promise not to give the children wine".

Griff's daughter Erie, aged three. Later she devoted her life to him.

Katie, a soldier's wife in Ipswich, with her two elder daughters.

Katie's photograph of Griff (right) and friends outside the Evans' quarters at Curragh Camp, Ireland.

Some of the servants who looked after the Evans family during their years in Madras.   118-119

The pony-trap (with syce) which overturned on Griff at Ootacamund.

Sylk's Hotel, Ootacamund, where Katie gave birth to a much-wished-for son.

The ayahs who looked after Katie's babies at   134-135
Ootacamund.

Indian street scene in the late 1870's—a snap from Griff's Indian scrapbook.

Evans jolted over thousands of Indian miles in almost springless vehicles of this kind.

Katie with Griff in the garden at Brynkynallt,   166-167
Bangor.

Griff in his study. His gesture of deafness— cupping his ear with his hand— was characteristic.

Ellen: A girl of spirit and a born nurse.

Griff in the drawing room at Brynkynallt.

"I am determined to walk again and take little   182-183
grandson Griff on my *good* knee."

When they discovered the old doctor up the hill was a scientist of international repute they gave him the Freedom of the City.

A specimen of Griffith Evans' handwriting in his 90s. Later, the then Duchess of York showed one of his letters to Princess Elizabeth, remarking: "Isn't it a simply marvellous piece of penmanship, for a man in his hundredth year?"

CHAPTER ONE

Prelude by Jean Ware

The Centenarian

I woke at dawn. Healthy girls who love sleep rarely see the rising sun, but I had to be at my grandfather's house by seven to help Aunt Erie prepare for his hundredth birthday, and it was a long walk from our house on the shores of the Menai Straits to the steep hill on the other side of Bangor.

This was not just a centenary celebration. Griffith Evans, my mother's father, had been discovered in old age, hailed by the newspapers as "the scientist the world forgot," and given the freedom of the city.

At twenty, I found it hard to imagine what it must feel like to look back on a hundred years of life. When my grandfather was born, William the Fourth was on the Throne; our last battle had been Waterloo; people still travelled in stage coaches; doctors used leeches. Now, a century later, the life of King George the Fifth was moving towards its close; Baldwin had begun to arm against the Nazis; the horse had almost been pushed off the road; Alexander Fleming had discovered penicillin. My grandfather had lived through the Crimean War, the American Civil War, the Franco-Prussian War, the Boer War, the Great War and the Russian Revolution. And only last Sunday the old man had said, "This Hitler will bomb us all in our beds."

I searched in the wardrobe for my Greta Garbo flat shoes, and paused at the mirror to give my shoulder-length hair a last curl inwards in imitation of the Swedish idol of my generation. Then I crept downstairs and went out. The summer sunshine was sliding down the Straits from Liverpool Bay, and in the morning stillness I could hear the plaintive cries of the oyster-catchers along the muddy shores.

For me and my sister and three brothers our grandfather was an institution. He always gave us a treat on his birthday, and paid for expeditions of our own choosing. He loved us as he loved his

1

Welsh terriers, with a continued practical concern for our welfare.

At eighty-nine he led us up the pedestal to the top of the Marquess of Anglesey's column, his legs in hairy tweed steadily mounting the steps - more than a hundred of them. Up there, we all sang "Land of my Fathers," as he gestured proudly towards the Snowdonian range. He sang the Welsh words with us, and although he was very much out of tune, he was not at all out of breath. He told us that this was because he had not touched a drop of alcohol or a cigarette all his life.

Every Sunday we trooped up the hill for tea with him. Like most North Wales children we called our grandfather "Taid" (to rhyme with "tide"). When I was small I was taught to speak into his ear which he would cup with his hand; he had been hard of hearing all his life. His loud, military voice was all the louder because he could not hear himself speak and had no idea he was shouting. One of the penalties of going with him to the kinema, as he called the "pictures", on a Saturday afternoon, was that not only did we have to yell at him but he shouted back at us, and our school friends up in the gallery revelled in the dialogue and did not hesitate to tease us the following Monday.

"Did your mother like the jam I sent her?"

"Oh yes, Taid, it was lovely!"

"Lovely is not a word you should apply to jam. A young girl may be lovely, but jam is delicious; jam is tasty."

And once, at a matinee of a romantic film, we nearly died of shame. Taid had imagined from a publicity photograph that this would be a film about whaling, and throughout all the close-ups of kissing he thumped his stick on the floor and bellowed, "This is ridiculous! Where are the whales?"

He used to walk his dogs every morning and take a "run" down Town Mountain "to keep my knees supple." But in his ninetieth year he tripped over a root and broke his leg. The ambulance men offered him brandy. He poured it over the grass, shouting, "Alcohol is poison!" He was determined to walk again, and after some weeks he did; but a second fall caused another break which would not knit, and for the past five years he had been bedridden.

He accepted his fate like the soldier he was. "What can't be cured must be endured," he said. The second accident mellowed him. It was after his enforced immobility that we, his grandchildren, really got to know him. Sitting up in bed, surrounded by the latest periodicals which he would annotate with a red pencil in a

2

firm, neat hand, a 200-watt bulb gleaming over his bald head, he was much more approachable than when he used to stride around with his magnificent military bearing, his stick, stentorian voice and best-quality Welsh tweed suits.

A year or two later he became totally deaf. He laid in a stock of little notepads which he kept by his bed for visitors. When we wrote on them our juvenile views of life, he would read them slowly and with interest through his magnifying glass; then, folding his huge, bony hands on the coverlet he would consider his reply. Nothing ever shocked him. He was one of the few in our Celtic world who treated all subjects unemotionally. He weighed the pros and cons as if we were visiting professors. Even when, at eighteen, I returned from Germany glowing with enthusiasm of life in a German Maidens' Camp and ardently pro-Nazi, he did not try to persuade me I was wrong. He asked many questions and peered thoughtfully at my answers. Then he dictated a list of articles and books I should read "as a background to what you have witnessed." He was then ninety-eight.

His birthday was as family-orientated for us as Christmas. But this 1935 birthday wasn't just a family occasion. We had to share him with the Royal Veterinary College who wanted to honour the father of their profession. Griffith Evans had been unearthed by the world five years before at the annual meeting of the British Association. He had been named by the President, who came from Pretoria, as the man who had first contributed to the discovery of the lethal significance of the tsetse fly, and thus, as he said, to "the opening up of Africa." When the President revealed that this scientist was still alive, Taid's house on the hill was besieged by newspapermen. They even came from America to interview the last man in Europe known personally to Abraham Lincoln. From being a local character - "the old doctor who used to be a colonel in the army" - Taid, in his nineties, was transformed into a figure of international fame.

I wished that Nain, my merry little grandmother, were alive to help us through this day. She had died twelve years before. She was the link between her husband and the many friends who came to their home. Their marriage was an attraction of opposites. Griff Evans was fair, bony, rigid and abrupt in movement and speech, utterly unlike the popular image of a Welshman. The early Scandinavian marauders round the coasts of Merioneth may have been responsible for his genes. Nain was dark, a compact, cuddlesome little person. Her eyes were receptive pools, as

3

brown as the backwaters of her own Montgomeryshire rivers. Griff's eyes were turquoise blue, as keen as swords. He put everything, including people, under his mental microscope. He analysed, judged and classified. Nain simply enjoyed people and their foibles. Griff was as philistine as she was artistic, but she put up with the *kitsch* he brought into the house and quietly popped things into the attic when he had forgotten about them. They were still in love when she died in her eightieth year.

I climbed the hill to Brynkynallt, the late eighteenth-century house, which my grandfather had bought in 1890 for his retirement from the army. I opened the garden gate and stood on the terrace high above the town. The morning sunlight burnished the bell-pull which would soon be tugged by the comers on this centenary day. Before noon, the sun would have disappeared behind Town Mountain, and the grey house would be in shadow. Griffith Evans liked it that way. When he bought the place he said to my grandmother, "This is the house for us! I've had enough sun in India to last me until I am a hundred!"

And now he *was* a hundred.

I looked up at his bedroom window. It was on a level with the top branches of the cherry trees, where now the birds were twittering. It was sad that he who so loved birds was unable to hear them. Nor could he hear the Cathedral bell ringing for early service, or the milkmen in High Street below clattering their cans. When the bell stopped, the town clock struck seven, and I went into the house.

The entrance hall of Taid's home was so crammed with souvenirs of his hundred years that it looked like a museum. I walked between Welsh dressers, oak sideboards and ostlers' cupboards from his forebears' farm in Merioneth, past the exhibits on the walls: Indian pig-stickers, Zulu spears, collections of swords, sharks' teeth, elephants' tusks, tigers' claws, reindeers' antlers, stuffed birds, Persian rugs, a papoose-carrier which Taid had been given by a tribe of Sioux Indians, and a cone-shaped chair in which Nain had been carried over the Khasi hills.

My aunt came out of the dining room to meet me. Her face was pale and strained. When her father broke his leg the second time, she gave up the work she loved as Cardiff's first woman doctor, and came to look after him. We were all devoted to Aunt Erie and were sorry she was afflicted with such an odd name. She said:

"Taid was chatting till midnight with Sir Frederick."

I knew that she meant Sir Frederick Hobday, principal of the

4

Royal Veterinary College, who had come from London for the centenary, and that "chatting" meant Sir Frederick writing on the pad and Taid booming out his replies. I asked if Taid were exhausted.

"Not a bit, but I'm sure Sir Frederick was! He said Father had the virility of a superman. Oh dear," sighed poor Erie, pressing her forehead for a moment on my shoulder. "I shall be glad when today is over. Anything could happen."

Then she asked me briskly to sit with my grandfather for a while.

I went into the bedroom.

Taid was propped up with pillows, his long Viking head bent slightly forward, like a resting warrior. The bones of his face had strength and dignity. His eyes, half closed, gazed at some faraway scene beyond the bedroom wall. His gnarled hands were inter-locked. I was sure that they could still operate with care and tenderness on a suffering animal. His thumbs stood out like spatulas. He could have sat thus as a model for Rodin, a thinker ruminating at the end of his days, or a soldier collecting himself for a rendezvous.

His turnip watch ticked on the bedside table. He was always time-conscious. I picked up the visitors' pad on which everyone wrote messages: the whole family had become facile at this means of communication. I read my aunt's note written the night before: "Sian is coming early, and I will come to you at 7.30".

My grandfather always called me Sian, the Welsh for Jean. I flicked back the pages. A couple of days ago my mother had sat with him, and as he dozed she had composed some verses. I thought them too good to leave on the pad and be thrown away. I tore out the page and tucked it into my bag.

Taid became aware of me; he turned his head and his face lit up.

"Hey, hey, Sian," he hailed me in his tremendous voice. He raised both hands beckoning towards his chest in his characteris-tic gesture of welcome. I put my hand between his great paws and nodded into his face and he knew I was wishing him a happy birthday.

"Have you had your breakfast?" he demanded, as if I were at the other end of a parade ground. I shook my head. "Then you must go down and let Annie give you some eggs and bacoh."

I wrote that I would prefer to stay with him and begged him not to talk but to rest in preparation for the afternoon. He studied

5

this carefully, then replaced the pad and laid his magnifying glass beside it. Without comment he folded his hands and resumed his position of repose.

On the table was the usual pile of newspapers and periodicals with which he kept himself up to date. One, with a marker stuck in it, was the "Veterinary Record" for that week. He had been reading an editorial tribute to himself:

No account of Griffith Evans' life and work could be written without evoking that almost breathless interest so frequently associated with fiction. Had there been no Evans the scientist, Evans the man must have made his name. Else how could he in person have persuaded Abraham Lincoln himself to make an exception in his favour when authority in Washington point-blank refused access to the American Civil War front to Commanders of Guards, medical and other officers, heaven knows how high? And the encounter with General "Beast" Butler, too. How would a less amazing personality have dealt with him?

Human tuberculosis and tetanus, anthrax and surra in India - he left the mark of his brilliant, virile brain upon them all. Possessed of the ruthless determination of the pioneer, yet sweetened with the thirst for knowledge and a love of his fellow men of rare quality, so that he could see others at work of lesser scientific merit and lauded to the skies without bitterness at his own relative lack of recognition: here is one whose character and achievement in his chosen ways may well stand as an example to veterinarians for all time.

How wonderful, I thought, to live to be a hundred and read such a tribute on one's birthday morning! For years the people of Bangor had no idea that the old doctor up on the hill was one of the pioneers of modern medicine. Bangor was thousands of miles from the scorched plains of the Punjab, and half a century away from the Afghan War when Griffith Evans, as inspecting veterinary surgeon in the army, was sent to the North West Frontier to investigate a disease which was ravaging the horses. What he discovered is now part of scientific history.

My aunt came into the room.

"Two more telegrams," she said, "One from Cousin Elsie Dyffryn Ardudwy, and the other from the Prince of Wales."

I giggled at the juxtaposition, but she was too flustered to see the funny side. She laid the telegrams on Taid's coverlet and he said: "I hope you gave the telegraph boy a glass of lemonade for climbing the hill?"

Erie nodded at him and spoke to me: "He refused it - said he never drinks anything but beer, and he well knows he won't get *that* in this house!"

I went downstairs to help Annie and the morning passed quickly. I hoped the ceremony would start on time. Taid was such a stickler for punctuality. In our childhood he would arrange to meet us outside the "kinema" at twenty two and a half minutes past two precisely. He would stand there holding his enormous watch as we tore down the road towards him. "Bravo!" he would say. "Only thirty seconds - or five seconds - or two seconds - late this time!"

But the hands of his watch pointed to exactly 2.30 when the party gathered round Taid's bed. Only a few could be squeezed into the small bedroom. I could see the crowd of civic and university dignitaries clustered below in the garden. People had climbed on to the railings and were standing all down the hill.

My eldest brother and I had been placed in the open dressing room door behind the bed, from which we could see the faces ranged in a respectful arc round Taid. I had a dreadful urge to giggle, but I was proud that they were making such a fuss over dear old Taid's birthday, which he usually spent alone while we all went out on a picnic at his expense.

The star performer, Sir Frederick Hobday, stood at Taid's left hand. Next to him was our Bangor vet, Mr Savage, known locally as "Savage the Animals". Beside him loomed the dark aloof figure of Uncle Goronwy, Taid's only son. Completing the semi-circle were my father, and, next to him, the Mayor, the Town Clerk and the Press: Mr MacDermid, the reporter, and a photographer. By craning my neck, I could almost read Mac's notes as he held his notebook over Taid's right ear. On chairs at the foot of the bed sat Taid's daughters: Wynona, Erie, Towena and my mother Mair, the youngest and gentlest of the four. Our aunts' names were something of a family joke. Wynona, meaning "eldest daughter", commemorated her father's friendship with a tribe of Red Indians. Erie was named after Lake Erie, recalling Taid's service in Canada. Towena was called after Towyn, his native village.

The three aunts, like their brother, wore secretive, wary expressions, and seemed on guard against each other. Only my mother smiled at us as we peeped from behind the bed. It was rare for them all to be assembled together. Each had pulled up a private drawbridge. I thought how remarkable it was that Taid had reached his century without losing one of his five children; but somehow his children had lost each other.

The little ceremony began.

Sir Frederick had prepared a short speech, and he gave a copy to Taid, who studied it carefully through his magnifying glass.

Sir Frederick said we had met to honour the father of the Royal Veterinary College and of the whole veterinary profession. He paused, picked up a frame containing a parchment, and told us that the frame had been made from wood taken from the College's original building in London where Griffith Evans was a student in the eighteen-fifties. Taid was the only man alive to remember the place as it was then. The parchment, signed by its president, Prince Henry of Gloucester, testified to the services which Griffith Evans had rendered to veterinary and human medicine "with high courage over a phenomenally long period."

Taid took the frame and everybody waited in strained silence while he scrutinised it. At last he looked around the room, raised his hands as if he were calling a vast audience to attention, and burst into speech.

In front of me Mr MacDermid's head jerked up in shock at the volume of sound which almost blew his notebook out of his hand. He must have expected the trembling voice of age. I could see that the Mayor, the Town Clerk and Mr Savage were all equally surprised by the strength of Taid's vocal chords. Mr MacDermid recovered himself, and his pencil flew over the page; and this is part of what he later sent to the newspapers:

Dr Evans astonished the small company by his eloquence. Without a single note, he spoke for exactly half an hour in tones which could be heard even in the road outside his residence, and adroitly turned from scientific subjects to indulge in humorous flashes with the skill and facility of the practised orator.

One minute his hearers were listening to the value of alkaloids and acids, then came a joke at the expense of a professor at the Veterinary College.

8

"I am overwhelmed by this special message from my old college," said Dr Evans. And with a twinkle in his eye he recalled the old Welsh proverb: "If you want glory, you must die." He gave a picture of the college and its lecturers in the days of the young Queen Victoria, and went on to speak of love in human beings and in animals.

Taid was in full flood when Bangor's acting postmaster came into the room to deliver a telegram. It was from King George and Queen Mary in the Royal yacht at Cowes. According to Mr Mac-Dermid's report: "This took the breezy centenarian by surprise and he showed it." But I thought it was the interruption rather than the telegram itself that surprised Taid. He laid the Royal message down beside him and resumed his oration.

When he had finished there was an odd silence. I could see that everyone felt emotional and nobody knew what to do next. Then the white-haired Mayor and his town clerk drew closer to the bed and each clasped one of Taid's hands without speaking. The three old men had known each other for many, many years. These were Taid's own people, representing the town he had lived in for nearly half his life. For the first time he broke down and gave a queer little strangled sob. It was agonising to see him trying not to weep. He said hoarsely, "I don't know what to say. I only wish my dear wife were with me to-day. She shared every-thing. Whatever I did in this town was due to her help."

It was over. Everybody went away.

That night, I sat in my bedroom window and watched the reflections of the sunset in the Straits. It had been a long day. I took out a crumpled piece of paper from my bag and read again the verses my mother had written in her father's notebook as she sat by his bedside a few days ago.

The old man dreams. The young ones watch and say:
"What does he do to pass the time away?"
They see the little room, the wooden bed,
The big white light that shines above his head,
The bedside clock, the bottles, books around,
No sound, no sun, only a peace profound.
"The old man dreams," they say. They little know
How that dim room is peopled and aglow

With phantom faces, pity, hopes and fears,
The living past of nigh a hundred years.
'Tis we are blind! The shadows come and go
And hold his hand and speak. We do not know.

It was a long sunset, and now it was almost dark. "The living
past of nigh a hundred years." If ever a man had a book in his life,
that man was my mother's father.

CHAPTER TWO

Boyhood in Wild Wales

Two years before Victoria became Queen, a generation before George Borrow wrote "Wild Wales", when Merioneth was wild indeed, Griffith Evans was born, on August 7, 1835, in a rambling farmhouse near Towyn. His father's farm, hemmed in by the Irish Sea, the Cader Idris mountains and the marshlands of Afon Dysynni, was sixteen miles from the market at Machynlleth, and a very much longer ride from the nearest big town, which was Shrewsbury.

An Evan or a Griffith had farmed the land since about 1730 when Evan ap Jenkin came up from the south. He leased three hundred and sixty-three acres near Towyn and bought a further twenty-three on which he built a grey stone house, filling it with the oak furniture he had brought with him on a procession of carts. It was typical that he should call his home Tŷ Mawr, which means Big House, for the family always had a good opinion of themselves, and by local standards it was a big house with a huge kitchen and many small rooms. The big kitchen was the scene of Griff's earliest memory:*

> I used to stand on the oak settle in front of the fire to be rubbed dry after being lifted out of the bathtub. I was fascinated by the firelight shining on the polished oak and the brass knobs of the dresser. I remember the song one of the maids used to sing to me in Welsh:
>   Little Griff and I
>   Are going to London on the first of May.
>   The water is cold and the way is long.
>   Better for us to stay at home!

---

* This is one of the recollections of childhood which Griffith Evans recounted in old age. The song belonged to the time when travellers preferred to go to London by sea rather than overland from Merioneth.

11

Throughout his life Griff's mind was suffused with memories of his childhood at Tŷ Mawr. In old age he talked nostalgically of his winters there: lanterns swinging in the stableyard when guests arrived for the feast of St Cadfan or for Christmas; riding round the farm or driving to market with his father; standing on a stool to comb his mother's hair, or helping her to make treacle toffee. And the summers: the haymaking, the excitement of the hiring fair, chasing his terriers on the hills, seeing a barefist fight behind the Raven Inn.

Griff idolised his father. Evan Evans and his son became friends and companions from the moment the toddler could be lifted on to a pony's back. Evan was truly a man for all seasons. Powerfully built, he was a capable farmer. He was intelligent and well-read, schooled in Shrewsbury, fluent in the "fine tongue" and a sensitive, disciplined poet in Welsh. He was tolerant, describing himself as a "freethinking follower of Christ, going to the church of my father and the chapel of my mother as to two equal houses of God." He was honest and loyal; everyone respected his word. Griff was too young to see any fault in this benign, even-tempered man, who gave so freely to the local poor, who sold his produce cheaply, and was lenient with debtors; too young to detect the vanity, complacency, the desire for universal acclaim, the instinct for compromise which were compounded in his father's character. It was this wish of Evans to please everyone that was to bring him to ruin.

Possibly the boy and his father were drawn the closer together because Tŷ Mawr was so full of women: Griff's mother, his two aunts, two sisters, a governess and several maidservants, and a most formidable lady, his father's mother, Mary Evans. Her strong personality was a local legend. To wed Evan's father she had driven over from Montgomeryshire with a splendid dowry of three thousand golden sovereigns in a wooden box in her gig.

Mary made it a condition of her marriage that she should be allowed to found a congregational chapel in Towyn. She was a dissenter, and her antagonism to the Anglican Church had been intensified when a parson arrived in a drunken stupor to shrive her dying father. She insisted that her grandchildren attend Sunday school at her chapel, even though her son still kept one foot in the parish church.

Griff's mother, also called Mary, was an emotional, possessive woman and a zealous housewife. It is hard to imagine how the two matriarchs could share the same kitchen. The younger Mary spoke only Welsh and read no book but the Welsh Bible. She was quick-tempered, but Griff and his sister Maria rarely incurred her anger. Her son could do no wrong, and Maria, two years older, was a gentle girl. Eliza, however, two years older again, was a rebel, strong-willed like her grandmother. It was not infrequently her fate to be flung across her mother's knee and spanked on her bare bottom. Griff remembered one such occasion in particular:

One day Eliza defied Mother in front of the farm hands in the yard, actually pulling a face at her. Mother had been tidying her garden, of which she was very fond, and she seized a thick bunch of nettles and thrashed Eliza with them. Eliza then stuck her tongue out. Mother became very angry and took up a holly branch she had just pruned and whipped Eliza until her botty bled. "*Now* will you do as you are told?" she cried, but Eliza, howling with pain, stamped her foot and shouted "No!" Maria and I stood holding hands and we were very frightened when Mother hauled Eliza indoors and locked her in the dark cellar to await Father's return. I was glad that Father came in soon afterwards and carried Eliza upstairs, saying she had been punished enough.

There were few children for Griff to play with in easy reach of Tŷ Mawr. But it seems this serious-minded little boy never really learned to play at all. He preferred the company of older people, and spent much time with Robin, the chief *gwas*(farmhand), a great story-teller, who used to tell him how he had survived Waterloo by buying himself out of the army*. But it was his father who dominated most of Griff's early memories: those drives in the gig to Machynlleth Market, along the White Valley through the mountains, when Evan would make up Welsh verses; that late journey along the cliff road from Barmouth when the moon was reflected in a silver path across the sea:

No matter how fast the horse trotted, we could never leave

* Robin claimed he had bribed another man to take his soldier's uniform. The man was killed at Waterloo bearing Robin's name. "So I really don't exist!" he would say. He lived into old age at Tŷ Mawr.

the moonbeam behind. "Why does it keep following us?" I asked, and my father said it was because things are not always what they seem.

And when his father came to his crib to say goodnight:

"Why does my candle stay the same when it has given its light to your candle, Tada?" Father said it was because goodness could give itself away and never become less.

But the more practical turn of Griff's mind began to show when he was very young:

While my father was composing a poem about snow and frost coming to the mountain Yr Aran, as we drove along to market, I looked back at the Towyn marshes and wondered why in summer so many mosquitoes danced down there while here on the moors there were so few. The old people who lived on the marshland complained of the ague and said it came from the mosquitoes.

Forty years later, Griff was to recall that folklore, on the North-West frontier of India, with the stench of dead horses in his nostrils.

Evan found a well-educated Welsh girl, Miss Mair Pugh, to ground his children in English, Welsh, arithmetic and "the use of the globes, terrestial and celestial, to explain the universe". He did not have them baptised, either in church or chapel, saying they must be free to choose their own faith.

Father's best friend among the county people was his liberal-minded landlord, Captain Edward Scott, who had been an equerry to William IV. He used to take me to visit him at his house, Bodtalog, and I remember sitting on the floor leaning against his knee and looking at cartoons in "Punch". I wore my best homespun dress, so I must have been less than five or six years old, when boys went into trousers. My mother called it my "crimsi" as it was woven in squares of grey bordered in crimson. Almost everyone then wore locally-woven homespun in a variety of six basic colours.

Griff's first pair of trousers were made by the travelling tailor who took in Tŷ Mawr on his round of farms and manor houses.

The tailor would sit cross-legged on the table, sewing and spreading the latest gossip. It was during one of these visits, when I was recovering from scarlet fever, that my mother realised my hearing had been affected, because I kept asking him to repeat what he had said.

This was the start of a lifelong handicap. Griff acquired the habit of cupping his ear with his hand in an effort to hear, a gesture which became part of him.

He was early indoctrinated against strong drink by his implacable grandmother who regarded alcohol as one of the most sinful manifestations of perfidy. She was supported, more tolerantly, by his father: Evan was not averse to an occasional glass of port, but he founded the Towyn Temperance Society and was chairman of the Rechabite group, thus he must have been well pleased when Griff, still in petticoats, came home from Sunday School to announce that the Rechabite officials had asked him to be "treasurer."

My duties were quite simple: I had to collect farthings from the farm servants at Tŷ Mawr, which would be an insurance for them in need and misfortune. I undertook this task with much seriousness, and I recall sitting on a stile on the way home from Sunday School while my sisters taught me how many farthings there were in a penny. They did this by pointing to the squares on my "crimsi" which were divided into halves and quarters.

Evan Evans was a liberal-minded man, a disciple of William

15

Cobbett. He prided himself on his rationalism and independence of mind. The countryside was rife with superstition which he detested, and he strove to protect his children from being influenced by supernatural fears.

When the Vicar of Towyn died, my father told Ann, our nursemaid, to dress me and my sisters in our best clothes and take us to view his body, which in those days was a mark of respect and even children were expected to do it. Ann told us we must be sure to take hold of Vicar Edwards' big toe. When Eliza demanded to know why, she replied, "So that you will never see his ghost." When we arrived at the bier, Eliza lifted me up so that I could pinch the dead man's toe. It felt like a lump of wood. On the way home, Ann said that when Vicar Edwards died, the effigy of Griffith ap Adda * in St Cadfan's Church was seen to weep real tears. My father laughed when I repeated Ann's words, and some time later on a wet day he took me into the church in Towyn to see the moisture in the knight's eye. He explained it was simply the result of condensation in humid weather. "You must always look for a rational reason for silly stories," he said. And I have always done so.

In those days Wales had its witch doctors or specialists in magic. They were known as "cynjars". They foresaw the future, made potions to cure sickness in men and beasts, and produced love spells.

My father was indulgent towards our local cynjar, a kindly old man who, when he was dying, produced his book of 365 spells saying, "You once did me a great kindness, Meistr Evans, and this is the best I have to give." But he was roused to anger by another cynjar, an apothecary - and actually a deacon in a chapel- who sold worthless prescriptions for sick animals at Machynlleth market, and also covertly retailed charms and spells to keep evil at bay. His hypocrisy in sitting in the deacon's seat in chapel, when he knew he could be

*Griffith ap Adda, a knight at the court of Edward III, was one of the Evans family ancestors. His effigy in the parish church is known as the Weeping Warrior.

excommunicated for dabbling in magic, was pointed out to me by my father. We used to call him Mr Humbug.

I remember once how, out of the kindness of his heart, my father went over to spend the night with an old farmer and his wife near Aberdovey. They had complained that their house, Penhelyg, was afflicted with a poltergeist. There were strange noises at night as if crockery were being thrown about, and the old pair were getting no sleep. Father offered to sit up in the kitchen so that they might have one night's sleep without fear, as, like most country folk at that time, they really believed in ghosts. He worked all night preparing his lessons for the next Sunday school, the Bible open on the table. When the farmer later reported that no more had been heard from the poltergeist, the whole neighbourhood was convinced that it had been exorcised by the open Bible. But my father impressed upon me that this was a case of pure coincidence.

Although Evan Evans liked to keep in with the Anglican Church, the church of the gentry, his sympathies were with the dissenters. He often provided hospitality for travelling evangelists.

On one occasion I was told to ride into Towyn and ask that the town crier be sent out to announce the unexpected visit of a famous preacher, and that the minister should open the chapel for him.

After the service, Griff's father would invite his farm workers and maids to meet the preacher round the kitchen fire.

They would ask him many questions. The Bible, the chapel and the preachers supplied the drama in their lives. They knew no other library, theatre or actors.

John Humphreys, the old shepherd of Tŷ Mawr, was a lay preacher and one day, when out on the sheep walk, Griff heard his voice borne on the wind, declaiming a sermon to his ewes.

17

The following Sunday I went with my father to the Congregational chapel to hear John preach, and great was my surprise when the old man pointed a shaking finger at my father and accused "the dear Master there" (Meistr anwyl acw) of breaking the commandment "Remember the Sabbath to keep it holy." Father had allowed washing to be left hanging outside Tŷ Mawr all the previous Sunday! It mattered not that the garments were few in number. It mattered not that there had been heavy rain which had wetted them. The dear master should have sent out the womenfolk to bring them in. He should not have risked offending the Lord's commandment.

On the way home I asked Father if he were angry with old John for denouncing him in public. "Not in the least," my father said. "He has always prided himself on speaking his mind from the pulpit. I admire him for it, although I do not agree with his views. Years ago he preached against your grandfather, when corn was reaped on a fine Sunday during a wet spell. Like you I asked my father if he were angry, and this is what he said to me: 'To everyone freedom of opinion, and to every opinion a voice.' And that is what I say to you now. If we had a family motto, that should be it."

Of all the events of my childhood, I think this walk home with my father made the deepest impression on me.

In 1846 life at Tŷ Mawr suddenly changed. First came the death of old Mary Evans. To Griff the loss of his Nain seemed like the end of an era. Then in September a British school was opened at the hamlet of Bryn Crug nearby, and Griff was entered as one of the first pupils. Meanwhile, his sisters were to go to boarding school, and Miss Mair Pugh left to take up another situation. Griff missed the governess even more than he missed his grandmother. She had taught him well and to her he owed his clear script, his lucid Biblical English and his dexterity with figures. She had also developed his love of reading.

Eliza was now fifteen and Maria thirteen. They were to ride in charge of a groom to a boarding school in Hereford. Griff admired Eliza, his purposeful elder sister who rode her pony fearlessly, stood up to everyone, and was inclined to be bossy with him. But he loved Maria, and found it hard to see her go.

Three bad portraits painted at this time by a travelling artist show Griff's mother and father sitting straight and stern in profile, mother in a mob cap, father looking self-satisfied and very much the country gentleman; and Griff himself in full face, a fair-haired boy with a Byronic open collar. His nose is big, his mouth small. His best features are his determined chin and his honest, searching blue eyes, having in them a suggestion of loneliness.

I felt lonely after my sisters had gone . . . I missed Maria very much and was delighted when her letters began to arrive. One was written on elegant notepaper bearing a picture of the new Rotherhithe tunnel. She began, "O how joyful it shall be to see my brother at Nadolig" (Christmas) – but her English was not good and she soon lapsed into Welsh.

Even if he had been more inclined to make friends among the boys at the Bryn Crug British School, Griff was set apart by being the son of the biggest local farmer, and by having to help the underpaid schoolmaster to teach English to the other children. He was asked to do this because he was probably the only thoroughly bilingual boy in the school. His lack of companions, his disinterest in children's games, may be explained partly by his natural diffidence but mostly by his upbringing, by his father's desire to have him as a companion and to treat his son as a grown man while he was still a child. And it was no doubt to encourage him to accept responsibility that, when he was scarcely twelve years old, Evan asked him to ride into Machynlleth with a bag of gold to take to the bank. It was a long journey for a boy, and in those days not without its dangers. The farm servant, Robin, was concerned for Griff's safety.

While Robin was helping me to saddle my pony he warned me that if I met a robber I was to remember the stories he had told me about Twm Sion Catti * and to use my wits to get the better of any bad man. I took heed, but my ride was uneventful.

---

* The Robin Hood of Wales.

19

Probably sensing his son's loneliness, Evan gave Griff two Welsh terriers. Never before or afterwards was he so devoted to any animals.

I have never ceased to long for the two little dogs, Terra and Snap, I had as a boy. I left them when I went to London. They were both faithful and I shall ever be grateful to them. While I remember them I cannot doubt that dogs do reason, and I am quite willing to believe they have souls. I should think all the better of heaven if I found that Terra and Snap had preceded me.

In his fourteenth year, he was sent to a school at Pennal on the road to Machynlleth. He lodged in the village and came home for weekends. Usually his father or Robin would meet him on horseback, leading his pony. It was on these walks and rides that he saw something of the dire poverty of the Hungry Forties.

Once I came upon a small boy weeping on the side of the road. He had been sent out to beg, and his voice rose to a wail as he told me he was lost, cold and hungry. I carried him piggy-back home to Tŷ Mawr where my mother comforted him. Another day I heard a frail old voice singing a Welsh hymn on the other side of a hedge, and found a starving tramp. Some people were rendered too weak from starvation to stir out at all. One day I went with my father to the cottage of two old weavers who had not been seen for some days. We found them in bed, almost in a coma. My mother and one of our maids nursed them back to some strength. There was an order that people must not seek work outside their own parish for fear of increasing the burden of other districts. My father was prevailed on to protest about this. A man in the last stages of exhaustion arrived at Tŷ Mawr saying he had walked to South Wales and back vainly seeking work. My father engaged him for his keep and a shilling a day. His name was Hugh Gabriel and he stayed on as one of our most loyal servants for over twenty years.
The constant stream of beggars pleading for food at the farms distracted the farmers' wives, and at a meeting held by

20

the farmers it was decided to receive beggars on one day of the week only. This was fixed for Wednesday for the Towyn area. On Wednesdays I would sometimes help to hand out measures of wheat and barley to the hungry men and women who came to Tŷ Mawr. They would then take the grain to the local miller who ground it free of charge.

When Griff left school in the summer of his seventeenth birthday he worked with his father on the farm. But he became restless and began to have doubts about being a farmer all his life. Evan, a little worried, sent him off alone to spend a night in Shrewsbury and make some purchases for the farm, thus hoping to satisfy Griff's desire to see the world. He was even to take a short ride on one of the new railway trains. Hugh Gabriel had done this and described it:

Like flying it is. Like the wind. You see a tree through the window, and before you can look at it, it is gone.

Griff was disappointed in the train ride, which seemed to him "less exciting than a good gallop". Far from curing his wanderlust the sights of Shrewsbury made him long to see more distant places, and hearing so much English spoken all round him gave him the thrill of being in a foreign land.

He became friendly with the young Aberdovey physician, Dr John Pughe, for whom he sometimes delivered medicine to remote farms. He gained hints on the treatment of sick animals, and heard stories about life at St Thomas' Hospital, London, where Pughe had qualified. One day he told his father that he would like to become a doctor.

Reluctantly, because for Evan it must have been a severe blow that his only son should not want to farm the land of his forebears, the father agreed that Griff as a first step should be apprenticed to Dr Pughe.

One of Pughe's patients was the vicar of Towyn, the successor to Mr Edwards. He was an alcoholic in the last stages of *delirium tremens*. Griff offered to sit up with him.

I felt a deep pity for him, knowing that it was loneliness after

21

his wife's death which had started him drinking. I sat with him for three nights, and then for the first time I witnessed a man's death. His sufferings set the seal, if I needed one, on my vow of total abstinance.

While he was working for Dr Pughe - and probably under his influence - Griff showed the first signs of his life-long interest in the nature and circulation of blood. He persuaded his father to let him hasten the death of a dying donkey. He stunned it so it should feel no pain, then he strung it up in a barn and attempted to examine its still-beating heart. He shot the animal before it regained consciousness. It is doubtful if he learned much and he had to spend several hours cleaning up the mess.

Suddenly, fate struck a blow at the Evans family which affected the whole course of Griff's life. Evan's brother John suffered from delusions of grandeur and always sought to impress the local gentry. He had embarked on wildly ambitious schemes to improve his wife's estates at Abermad. Evan had guaranteed him against debt, giving his surety almost light-heartedly, never suspecting that anything could go wrong. But now, John was bankrupt. A lawyer's letter had arrived at Tŷ Mawr. The creditors were foreclosing on Evan's security, demanding the money forthwith.

This was a disaster. Evan had always aspired to buy the land he farmed when the lease ran out in 1875. Now that ambition became an impossible dream. He would have nothing to leave his son but his farmhouse, and the mere twenty-three acres that he actually owned. Further, he would have to ask Griff and his sisters to part with the £3,000 they had from their grandmother.

Father looked white and ill. He explained to me and my sisters in the parlour what had happened. He asked us if we would go with him to the lawyer's office and sign away the inheritance we had each received from Nain Evans. For the sake of our father's honour we all three willingly agreed. But as it proved even this was not enough. Father had to sustain a debt for the rest of his life.

Clearly, Tŷ Mawr held no future for Griff now, nor could his

Brynkynallt, Bangor: Griffith Evans'
retirement home.

Jean Ware: "He always called me
Sian".

Griff receiving a scroll from the Royal
Veterinary College on his hundredth
birthday.

Silhouettes of Griff aged 14 and his sister Maria.

Griff's father, Evan Evans. "His wish to please everyone was to bring him to ruin".

Right: Griff as a schoolboy.

Towyn as Griff knew it in the mid-nineteenth century.

father afford the cost of his training to become a doctor. Dr Pughe suggested that instead he should take the diploma of the Royal Veterinary College, which needed only two years' study if he worked hard. Evan wrote to the principal of the college, who replied, urging immediate registration, as already the first term of the college year had gone by; otherwise Griff would delay his examinations by a whole year. By the time this letter reached Tŷ Mawr, the last date for registration was almost upon them, and Griff must leave for London within a couple of days.

On a bitterly cold December night in 1853, I packed my bags in the little room where I had slept since I was two. I was to ride off with my father before daybreak in order to catch the stage-coach from Machynlleth to Shrewsbury, and he would take my pony back home on the leading rein.

When Mother bent over me with a candle at four in the morning, she said that a blizzard was blowing and the snow was already deep around. There would be drifts in the road through the White Valley. Father and I rode out of the farmyard, with only Robin there holding a lantern and wishing us godspeed. More than once we had to dismount and lead our horses through the drifts. Sometimes we were waist deep in snow. The struggle was exhausting.

They reached Machynlleth with only a few minutes to spare, both soaked to the skin. Evan hurried down the street in search of dry socks for Griff. He hurled a pair of worsted hose through the window as the stagecoach moved out of the inn mews. As it jolted over the snowbound roads one of his father's poems ran through Griff's mind in rhythm with the striving horses in the swirling snow:

> Pob un red, pawb yn ei rwn - a'r risiau
> Yr oesoedd cyflymwn.
> I fedi yr ynfudwn.
> Byd i hau, yw'r bywyd hwn.
> (Everyone runs, each in his own furrow; on the steps
> Of the ages we speed.
> To reap, we emigrate.

A life for sowing, this life.)

He reached Shrewsbury station just in time to catch the last
train to run on that line for a week.

CHAPTER THREE

A Student in Victorian London

In the grey light of a December morning, Griff presented himself at the Royal Veterinary College in Camden Town. This Welsh country boy had never seen a town bigger than Shrewsbury; his first impressions of London were so confused that he remembered only his astonishment at seeing so many horses in the crowded streets.

> The college was built in rectangular form, and when I entered the quadrangle, I saw a handsome stallion being walked up and down the flagstones. A friendly student, who had been observing the horse's fetlocks, came up to me and explained that they were testing for lameness. When I said I had come to register, he told me his name was Meyrick and offered to lead me to the office and later, perhaps, show me round the college.

In this way, Griff began a friendship that was to last seventy years. James Joseph Meyrick was himself to achieve fame in veterinary history in a career which ran remarkably parallel to Griff's, first in rural practice, and later in the army in Canada and India. But in temperament they were very dissimilar. Meyrick, who was born in London, was different, sensitive, diplomatic and subtly humorous: characteristics which Griff markedly lacked.

Later Griff met Charles Spooner, the Principal, a staunch believer in the dignity of the veterinary profession which, he said, "has passed from the forge and farriery into the pharmacy, the dissecting room and the lecture hall . . . and has become part and parcel of the British and Indian army." This was a somewhat rosy view. The status of the profession was still recovering from the damaging regime of the notoriously ignorant Edward Coleman, an earlier principal of the college. Very much a "forge and far-riery" man, he thought the best vets were recruited from the stables.* Veterinary science was still in a primitive state. The college did not provide a microscope for the use of students. A paragraph in "The Veterinarian", which asserted that "many diphtheria cases occur between one and two a.m. because of exposure to night air", speaks eloquently of the standard of human and veterinary medicine in 1854.

Nevertheless, the college curriculum must have sounded very grand to the eighteen-year-old Griffith Evans, who was told that he would be taught "the anatomy, physiology and pathology of the horse, ox, sheep, pig and dog and of the domestic animals generally"; that he must study veterinary medicine and learn something of veterinary law. In addition, he must acquire a facility for shoeing horses. These subjects, the college said, would be outlined in lectures and, for the rest, the student must fill in for himself, because the professors did not believe in spoon feeding. In Griff's own words:

> I felt like a baby who had come to the college for food but found not only that I had to crawl after the food but even had to cook it for myself.

The regime was not rigorous. There were lectures between nine and four, and, if they wished, the students could continue working in the library and dissecting room till five. Unlike the other students, who were mostly out to enjoy themselves, several having patrons who would buy them commissions in the cavalry, Evans and Meyrick worked hard and rarely missed a lecture or dodged a dissection exercise.

> They called us "sweats", but, having missed a term, I was anxious to catch up. Every week I spent in lodgings was at the expense of my father who was also paying a substantial sum in fees.**

* In 1854 the Queen would not receive veterinary surgeons at levees and "Punch" depicted them as H-dropping characters in loud check suits.

** Twenty guineas a year.

Griff retained vivid memories of his professors and their eccen-
tricities. Charles Spooner, a humane and humorous man, was
forever dipping into his snuffbox. His speciality was horses and
his recurring theme was that nature was the best healer and that
sick animals had a natural tendency to recover. He was never
afraid to admit ignorance.

Once, during an epidemic of equine influenza, he asked his
class: "What is influenza?" A student said it was an influence. "But what is influence?" he asked. When the class
looked baffled he repeated the question: "Gentlemen, what
is influence?" Then, taking another pinch of snuff, he said
"God knows. I don't".

Professor James Simonds, a pioneer of anaesthetics in animal
surgery, specialised in diseases of ruminants and loved to dilate
on the value of mental rumination.

It was Professor Simonds who made me realise the importance of thoroughly masticating one's food. Adequate mas-
tication helps one to think clearly and prolongs life. Gobbled
food and confused thought go together.

As there was no microscope available for the use of students,
Professor Simonds advised Griff to buy one for himself.

"It will be your best friend," Simonds said, "but be careful of
the lenses and don't let any spittle fall on them." I bought a
microscope for £5 and a book explaining how to use it. A
new world opened up for me. I started with simple things,
noting the difference in the blood of various animal species,
observing in healthy animals the changes in blood before
and after feeding. I discovered the difference in ratio between red and white corpuscles.

Griff's fellow student must have regarded him not only as a

"sweat" but also as a prig as he displayed no interest in either girls or alcohol. He was, it seems, not so much annoyed as surprised when they imitated his Welsh accent. "I did not imitate their accent; why should they imitate mine?" Once Meyrick suggested that they should join a party of students who were going to a local music hall but he declined, saying that because of his poor hearing he would miss much of the fun.

He spent what leisure he allowed himself walking with Meyrick or alone. He had been pleased to find that London was not so claustrophobic as he had at first believed; that one could quickly escape into pleasant countryside; and, when spring brought blossoms to the trees, that even Camden Town retained something of its former rural character.

He lodged near the college in a house similar to that over which Mrs Pipchin presided in "Dombey and Son." It was one of a terrace of tall, thin houses with basements and above them rooms which became smaller the higher you went, until they tapered into several tiny attics, one of which he occupied. He spent winter evenings studying, his wrists kept warm by mittens knitted by his mother. He ate with the other lodgers in the basement. To save money, and for exercise, he walked everywhere rather than use the horse-omnibus. Sometimes, at the week-end, he and Meyrick liked to walk down to the Thames "which stank like the sewer it then was."

The London of 1854 was still very much the London of Dickens' "Christmas Carol". Griff had read of the evils of Dickensian London, but even so he was not prepared for the stench, the squalor, the debauchery which he found. He had seen poverty in Wales, but no child in Merioneth was left to starve and die of fever in the road, and young girls did not offer their bodies just to buy a crust of bread.

One night, returning from a walk in Westminster, he was stopped in Tottenham Court Road by a girl who plucked at his sleeve. She was pale and thin and scarcely more than fourteen. She asked him for sixpence and nodded towards a dark alley.

I did not understand what she meant. I asked what she would do with the money. She replied that she would buy food with it. I had only sixpence and some pennies. I gave her the sixpence and told her to get herself a meal.

28

He remembered this incident because shortly afterwards he had come upon a man with a telescope who was inviting passers-by to look at the stars.

I parted with my last few pence, the man saying that if I looked closely I would see the rings of Saturn.

The college encouraged students to visit the Zoological Gardens in Regents Park. Here Griff and Meyrick spent many happy hours. Often they went to see the livestock at the Metropolitan Cattle Market which the Prince Consort had recently declared open in the Caledonian Road.

One of Griff's memorable excursions was to the Great Exhibition in the gigantic glass house which had been moved from Hyde Park to South East London. His lifelong possessions included a simple souvenir which he bought there: a penny postcard that appealed to his somewhat naive sense of humour. It depicted a venerable man with a background of books, and was inscribed, "A learned man at present I appear, but turn me round, and lo! an ass is there." Upside down, the scholar vanished and the head of an ass stared out.

In the long summer evenings he and Meyrick went further afield; often to the lanes and heathland of Highgate and Hampstead.

I was moved more than once to shout at drivers on Highgate Hill for overloading their drays and lashing their struggling horses.

During these walks they talked of the Crimean War, of the rapid progress of British industry, symbolised by the Great Exhibition, of the growing schism between science and narrow orthodoxy. Meyrick was an agnostic and his heresies evoked a sympathetic response from Griff. They both retained nostalgic memories of those strolls, during which they explored each other's developing minds - until the needs of their stomachs brought them down to earth.

That summer there was an outbreak of cholera ominously close

29

to Camden Town. Almost thirty years before Koch discovered the cholera bacillus, it was a matter of speculation as to how the disease was contracted. John Snow, a discerning Soho doctor, in whose area five hundred people died in ten days, blamed contaminated water and urged that a pump in Broad Street should be sealed off. His theory was not generally accepted. Inevitably panic spread faster than the dread disease. Students were advised to stay away from the worst affected areas. The outbreak ended as suddenly as it began.

Suffering from the strain of overwork and the general tension caused by cholera, Griff found his *hiraeth* unbearable. When his father sent him some money and urged him to return home for the last week of the vacation, he was glad to accept this excuse for leaving London.

After eight months absence he saw his native countryside with new eyes.

Tŷ Mawr seemed smaller. Father and Mother looked older. Maria was thinner. My sister Eliza had married a merchant seaman named Griffith Dedwydd and gone to live at Barmouth.

The next winter was one of the worst of the century. Griff in his icy attic must have reflected miserably on what his parents were going through on the storm-lashed west coast. During those bitter months he worked with unflagging energy. He spent his second Christmas in London, unable to afford either the time or the money to go home.

In May, 1855, he graduated. He reaped the reward of his hard work, coming out at the top of the list. It was an unprecedented achievement for a boy who was still only nineteen, within eighteen months of going to the college. His tutors particularly commended his dissertation on "The Diseases of the Alimentary Canal of the Horse", which had been submitted to the Veterinary Medical Association.

So Griffith Evans became a member of the Royal College of Veterinary Surgeons and was ready to practise. In the following October the college announced a new rule: in future, students must have reached their twentieth birthday at the time of the examination.

CHAPTER FOUR

The Vet's Assistant

When the wife of the Bridgnorth veterinary surgeon ushered her husband's new assistant into her parlour on a chilly September day in 1855, Griff was astonished that she should ring for a maid to put more coals on the fire. He was unfamiliar with the more genteel way of life in Victorian England, and, in one of his few recollections of this period, he wrote:

> My mother would never have dreamed of summoning a maid to perform such a trifling service.

It was with some reluctance that Griff had decided to become a rural vet in Shropshire. His ambition was to travel and see more of the world, and also to undertake some kind of research work.

> I was, however, uncertain where I wanted to go or what sort of scientific investigation I wished to pursue.

His mother had begged him to stay near home. He had returned from London to find her looking wan and prematurely aged. The anxieties of the hard winter had taken their toll of both his parents' health; he felt he could not desert them.

So, after the harvest, he obtained a post in Bridgnorth. His employer was a pleasure-lover, a great racing man who rarely missed a meeting, an extrovert who immersed himself in the social swim of the town and urged Griff to do likewise because it was good for business. His wife, Griff decided, was a snob who cherished the faith that she and her husband were numbered among the "quality" of Shropshire.

31

"My employer"* was clearly a popular and experienced veterinary surgeon, skilled in the treatment of horses in particular, and held in high repute by the gentry and wealthier farmers. He left the poorer farmers and the humbler horses to his assistant. Griff had a hard beginning to his working life. His employer fell ill and there was a serious outbreak of cattle disease. The new assistant had to work almost round the clock with little time for sleep or meals. It was not a happy period.

I had no practical experience as a qualified veterinary surgeon and all the time I was dealing with strangers. I believe I owed more to the knowledge I had gained at Tŷ Mawr than to the training at the Veterinary College.

But if Griff did not think much of Shropshire it is doubtful whether, at first, Shropshire thought much of him! He was, at this stage, a gawky young man with big hands, long arms and legs, and had probably outgrown his homespun suit. At the age of twenty his manner would be gauche and he would be lacking in finesse. When Shropshire farmers sent for their cheerful and worldly vet and found themselves confronted instead by this immature young man, they may well have had serious misgivings about entrusting their animals to his care and perhaps wished they had sent for the local blacksmith instead. Nevertheless, a year later, Griff's father, visiting Shrewsbury, was proud to hear his son well spoken of by two Shropshire farmers.

After the first two months, Griff received a letter which made life suddenly seem brighter. His friend, James Meyrick, had also obtained a post as an assistant vet and was working at Newtown, over the Welsh border. From then on the two young vets exchanged letters and met as often as they could. Meyrick wrote:

I saw a two-year-old colt on Saturday with a white worm lying between pupil and cornea in the aquous humour . . .

*Very little written material survives about this period in Evans' career - only some correspondence with Meyrick and memories dictated in old age. In this correspondence he referred to "my employer" without mentioning his name, but it was almost certainly Mr James Atcherley of St Mary's Street, who was the principal if not the only established veterinary surgeon in Bridgnorth at this time.

32

the eyesight being quite gone. The owner will not pay me to
lance the cornea and take the worm out. I shall try to make a
bargain with him. If he will not pay me I think I will do it for
nothing.

Griff replied that he, too, had encountered a farmer's mean-
ness and to prevent a heifer from further suffering had treated
the beast without charge but had been chided for his charity by his
employer.

In another letter Meyrick said he was annoyed with a farmer
who had declined his help, preferring his horse to be examined
by the blacksmith. A week later he wrote:

The horse with the poll evil, of which I told you, was cured
by the old blacksmith. I cannot find his mode of treatment.
It is, I believe, a secret in his family.

Griff always respected the practical common sense which most
blacksmiths showed in treating animals. They usually understood
nature's own way of healing. Throughout his life, Griff would say
that often all a sick animal needed was to be allowed to rest in a
dry, well-ventilated place with plenty of fresh water to drink.

During his five years in Bridgnorth Griff seems to have had no
female friends. His employer's wife had sought to involve him in
the social life of the town, but he had little taste for dances, soirees
or concerts. There was, it seems, a young woman in the vet's
house; Griff mentioned her to his elder sister, but later said he
lost interest when he noticed, as she went upstairs, a gaping hole
in her stocking. Eliza teased him with this, and said he looked at
girls as if they were specimens under his microscope.

He did in fact spend a great deal of time looking into his
microscope. He had developed a keen interest in entomology.

I also took lessons in drawing because my attempts to draw
insects were so poor. I sought out an art teacher who allowed
me to join his group of students. This was a pleasant and
useful experience.

33

James Meyrick, strong in the expression of his agnosticism, was interested in the study of comparative religion. Griff shared his interest and, indeed, pursued it throughout his life. They attended the services of various denominations and afterwards exchanged notes. Griff, for example, wrote:

There is a small group in Bridgnorth who call themselves Irvingites. They are experimenting with the "gift of tongues" and claim to be moved to speak by the Holy Ghost. What I heard at their meeting sounded more like gibberish than divine message.

It was during this period that Griff, while not going so far as to call himself an agnostic, developed the free-thinking ideas which he often propounded in later years. He believed in the teaching of Christ if not in His divinity. He disliked the idea of priesthood, and thought that man's need for faith could be satisfied by the Sermon on the Mount. His philosophy was in fact very simple until, in later years, it became tinged by mysticism.

Unlike Griff, Meyrick, during his years in Newtown, was interested in girls. Indeed, throughout his life he enjoyed feminine company, but was a natural bachelor, viewing matrimony with considerable trepidation. In 1859 he confessed, however, to Griff that he had been courting a Newtown girl, a Miss Bickersteth, whose parents were strict Methodists. When he informed them of his wish to marry their daughter, they had been shocked by his lack of Christian belief which he had felt honour-bound to confess. They told him that unless he was willing to accept the gospel of God's truth, he must not see their daughter again. The girl, supporting her parents, had accused him of endangering their mutual love for the sake of a spiritual void.

He sought Griff's advice - though it would be difficult to imagine anyone less well equipped to give counsel on such a problem. Griff recommended him to stand by his principles and break off the relationship. But the sensitive Meyrick, though seemingly anxious to avoid marriage, was reluctant to hurt the girl's feelings.

By a quirk of fate, Meyrick's romance with Miss Bickersteth was responsible for changing the whole course of the two young men's lives.

Meyrick wrote urgently to Griff suggesting a meeting in Ludlow. He had decided that the best way out of his dilemma was to leave the district. When they met in Ludlow he produced an announcement he had cut from "The Times", stating that her Majesty's regiments were in need of veterinary officers; candidates were invited to sit for an examination with a view to their being awarded commissions in the army.

Griff agreed that it seemed a golden opportunity and they both decided to try their luck. In due course they were invited to take the examination in London and, shortly afterwards, were informed that they had been accepted for commissioned service.

When the gazetted list appeared in "The Times," it was read with much surprise by the Rector of Bridgnorth who for some time had been trying to arrange for his son to be commissioned in the infantry. How was it, he asked, that the young veterinary surgeon, Mr Evans, had been able to obtain a commission in the Royal Artillery? Who was his patron?

It was explained to the Rector that the Crimean War had revealed the army's immediate need for more veterinary surgeons. Griffith Evans and James Meyrick had no patrons, but were among the first men to be given direct commissions in the British army as veterinary officers by examination.

There is no record of what passed between Meyrick and Miss Bickersteth.

The two assistant vets exchanged their shabby tweeds for the officer's uniform of the Royal Horse Artillery. They knew nothing about soldiering but were skilled horsemen and good shots. Both had matured and filled out during their five years on the Welsh borders; their physiques were well suited to military uniform. And when, on January 30, 1860, they reported for duty as Acting Veterinary Officers at Woolwich, they were greeted by Mr John Wilkinson who ruled over the headquarters of the army's veterinary service at the Royal Horse Artillery Infirmary. Mr Wilkinson, the Queen's Principal Veterinary Surgeon, did not wear uniform but strutted about the parade ground in a frock coat and top hat, like a superior station master. He turned out to be an unimaginative, strict, parsimonious and unpopular man, but Griff respected him.

I thought Wilkinson was an honest man, zealous in his determination to raise the status of veterinary service.

Griff liked the army from the start. The military mind was definite, precise and well-disciplined. There was a right way of doing everything. Black was black, and white was white, with no vacillating shades of grey. This was the life for him.

He had scarcely settled into his new routine when he received a pathetic letter from his mother, asking if it was, even now, too late for him to change his mind. She had been deeply upset when he first broke the news of his commission to her. She thought he was destined for a life of debauchery, low-living and drunkenness. In a letter, laboriously written in mis-spelled Welsh, Mary Evans said that she had scarcely slept or eaten since he left her, for worrying about the temptations to which he would be exposed.

That day I had cause to go to London and I decided to ask the advice of an elderly and seemingly friendly clergyman who sat opposite to me in the train. "Do you think," I asked, "that a young man has any chance of leading a clean life in the army?"

The clergyman must have been astonished at being asked such a question by a smart young officer. But his reply seems to have been well considered.

He answered: "I see no reason why any young man should not lead a good life if he is true to himself and has the strength of character to resist whatever taunts are thrown at him."

That evening, Griff wrote to comfort his mother, quoting the clergyman's words. Nothing, he said, would persuade him to touch alcohol. He would never associate with women of ill-repute. He would always remember the training she had given him. Finally, he told her that the officer who had introduced him to the mess, a fellow-Welshman, Major Phillips, was a deeply religious man, well-versed in the Bible.

It was, perhaps, a somewhat priggish letter but it had the desired effect, and a week or so later Evan Evans wrote, telling Griff that his mother was eating her food again and was much more reconciled to having a soldier son.

Griff might have further reassured his mother by telling her that the officers' mess at Woolwich bore no resemblance to the den of vice of Mary Evans' imagining. Richly furnished and possessing a wealth of silver plate, the mess was often the scene of huge meals for visiting Victorian celebrities when protocol of dress and behaviour was strictly observed. It represented a style of life very different from Griff's homespun upbringing. Indeed, he was never at ease in the mess; he was not a club man and had little taste for stag parties, bawdy songs and the imbecilities of junior officers.

He was soon to face the test of his teetotal pledge. At his first formal mess dinner, during the "sacred" rite of passing the port, he committed the sin of saying "No thank you", pushing the decanter firmly away from him in the wrong direction. Meyrick, who sat beside him, was aghast, nudged him and told him he must pass the port to the next officer. Griff obeyed.

Although he was doubtless ragged by the young officers for his abstinence, Griff's diaries and recorded memories show that he had plenty of friends at Woolwich. He confessed to having one enemy, Lieutenant Smith,* who apparently disapproved of people obtaining commissions other than by purchase. He took a personal dislike to Griff, submitting him to thinly-veiled insults. In later years, Griff liked to recall this feud because, as in all good Victorian stories, right triumphed in the end.

The reforms being carried out by the Duke of Cambridge, the Queen's cousin, who was now getting into his stride as Commander-in-Chief of the British army, were often the subject of discussion in the mess. Major Phillips warned Evans to avoid making any criticism of the Duke in the presence of Mr Wilkinson who basked in the C. in C.'s patronage. Phillips was himself no admirer of the Duke and he told Griff how they had come into conflict during an inspection. The Duke, who was in a bad temper, had made some unfair complaints about a junior officer.

"When I remonstrated with him," Phillips said, "he fired a volley of abuse and blasphemy at me which I found intolerable. 'Sir,' I said, 'I am responsible to you but I am also responsible to God and His orders are that His name is not

*Probably not his real name. Evans used the phrase ". . . whom I shall refer to as
. . .".

37

to be taken in vain.' Turning to the Colonel the Duke demanded: 'Who is this lunatic?' The Colonel replied: 'Your Royal Highness, Major Phillips is one of my best officers.' The Duke left without completing the inspection.

On Whit-Sunday, 1860, Griff himself experienced the wrath of the Duke of Cambridge while accompanying a troop who were moving to the new camp at Aldershot.

Just beyond Kensington I saw among the crowds of sight-seers an old gentleman in civilian dress: I noticed him because he was mounted on a magnificent horse. He beckoned to me and I went up to him. "Why don't you salute me?" he demanded. I replied, "I don't know why I should salute you. I don't know who you are." "I am your Commander-in-Chief," he shouted - then lapsed into some foul language. I rode on. He bellowed after me: "Go and tell your commanding officer he will have to answer for not calling the troop to attention when meeting me!"

"The old gentleman," as Griff described him, was then only forty years old but had a prematurely aged appearance. Griff was soon to learn that both he and his C.O. had failed in their duty to the Commander-in-Chief. His account continues:

The fact was that not one of us recognised him. An order from the War Office awaited our arrival at Aldershot calling on the CO to explain why the troop did not salute the Duke. The CO sent for me and asked what explanation I could give for not saluting when the Duke personally ordered me to. I replied, "Tell his Royal Highness that I did not recognise him in civilian clothes and he expressed himself in such bad language, cursing and swearing, that I thought he was a lunatic. I have no other apology." Later I was told that the CO had a wigging, but, as for me, I heard no more of it.

From Aldershot, where he stayed for some days, Griff sent his father a description of how the Hampshire village was being transformed into the headquarters of the British army. On every

38

The face of compassion. Griffith Evans at 76 photographed by his son.

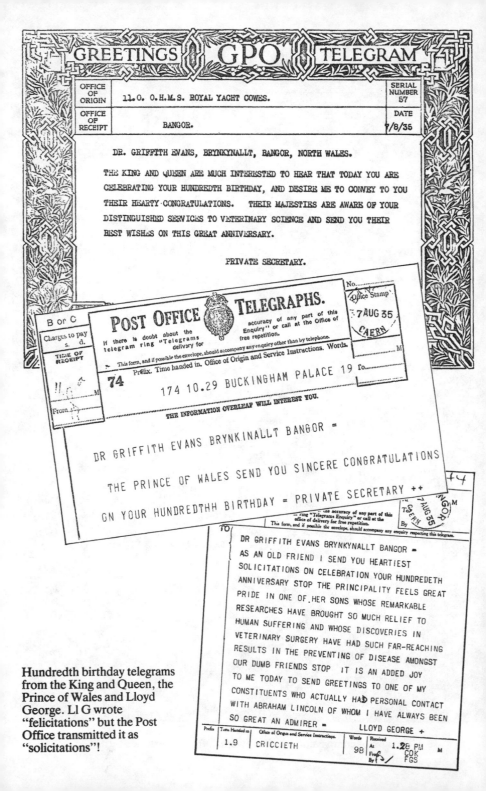

GREETINGS GPO TELEGRAM

| OFFICE OF ORIGIN | 11.0. O.H.M.S. ROYAL YACHT COWES. | SERIAL NUMBER 57 |
| OFFICE OF RECEIPT | BANGOR. | DATE 7/8/35 |

DR. GRIFFTH EVANS, BRYNKYNALLT, BANGOR, NORTH WALES.

THE KING AND QUEEN ARE MUCH INTERESTED TO HEAR THAT TODAY YOU ARE CELEBRATING YOUR HUNDREDTH BIRTHDAY, AND DESIRE ME TO CONVEY TO YOU THEIR HEARTY CONGRATULATIONS. THEIR MAJESTIES ARE AWARE OF YOUR DISTINGUISHED SERVICES TO VETERINARY SCIENCE AND SEND YOU THEIR BEST WISHES ON THIS GREAT ANNIVERSARY.

PRIVATE SECRETARY.

POST OFFICE TELEGRAPHS.

If there is doubt about the accuracy of any part of this telegram ring "Telegrams Enquiry" or call at the Office of delivery for free repetition.

This form, and if possible the envelope, should accompany any enquiry other than by telephone. Words.

Prefix. Time handed in. Office of Origin and Service Instructions.

74

174 10.29 BUCKINGHAM PALACE 19 to

THE INFORMATION OVERLEAF WILL INTEREST YOU.

DR GRIFFITH EVANS BRYNKINALLT BANGOR =

THE PRINCE OF WALES SEND YOU SINCERE CONGRATULATIONS

ON YOUR HUNDREDTHH BIRTHDAY = PRIVATE SECRETARY ++

DR GRIFFITH EVANS BRYNKYNALLT BANGOR =
AS AN OLD FRIEND I SEND YOU HEARTIEST
SOLICITATIONS ON CELEBRATION YOUR HUNDREDETH
ANNIVERSARY STOP THE PRINCIPALITY FEELS GREAT
PRIDE IN ONE OF HER SONS WHOSE REMARKABLE
RESEARCHES HAVE BROUGHT SO MUCH RELIEF TO
HUMAN SUFFERING AND WHOSE DISCOVERIES IN
VETERINARY SURGERY HAVE HAD SUCH FAR-REACHING
RESULTS IN THE PREVENTING OF DISEASE AMONGST
OUR DUMB FRIENDS STOP IT IS AN ADDED JOY
TO ME TODAY TO SEND GREETINGS TO ONE OF MY
CONSTITUENTS WHO ACTUALLY HAD PERSONAL CONTACT
WITH ABRAHAM LINCOLN OF WHOM I HAVE ALWAYS BEEN
SO GREAT AN ADMIRER = LLOYD GEORGE +

| Prefix | Term Handed in | Office of Origin and Service Instructions. | Words | Received At | 1.28 PM |
| | 1.9 | CRICCIETH | 98 | From By | COK FGS |

Hundredth birthday telegrams from the King and Queen, the Prince of Wales and Lloyd George. Ll G wrote "felicitations" but the Post Office transmitted it as "solicitations"!

side, he said, were expanses of dreary moor. The huts in the south camp for the use of those private soldiers permitted to have their wives and children living with them were appallingly over-crowded, ten married couples and a dozen or more children sharing an open hut, with blankets draped between the beds for privacy. In the village there had been a rapid growth of drinking dens and brothels. Griff saw six unfortunate soldiers doing pack drill as a result of drunkenness. Weighed down with heavy uniform and full marching kit they were compelled to march up and down in the summer heat for hours on end.

I wished I could have shouted to them to use their common sense and abstain from alcohol.

A week after his twenty-fifth birthday, in August 1860, Griff became officially a soldier of the Queen. His scroll, signed by her Majesty, read:

Victoria, by the grace of God of the United Kingdom and of Great Britain and Ireland, Queen Defender of the Faith, to our trusty and well-beloved Griffith Evans, Gentleman, greeting. We do by these Presents constitute and appoint you to be Veterinary Surgeon in our Royal Regiment of Artillery from the 31st of January 1860.
Given at our Court of St James' the Thirtieth day of August, 1860, in the Twenty Fourth year of our Reign.

In October, Griff was given leave and went home to Wales. His father had suggested that on his way to Tŷ Mawr he should break his journey at Llanfaircaereinion and, as an act of kindness, call on their old friends and kinsfolk, Dr John Jones and his wife Catherine, who were both in poor health. Griff knew that the doctor's chronic illness resulted from his heavy drinking and that his wife was suffering from anxiety over his alcoholism and the decline of his practice.

By the light of a hunter's moon Griff found the doctor's house and knocked at the door. It was opened by a girl with a lamp in her hand. It took Griff a few seconds to realise that this was Katie

Jones. When he had last seen her she was a lively little schoolgirl with a ready smile and - as his father said - a "jack-up nose." Now, almost seventeen years old, she had become a beautiful young woman, dark-haired and with warm sympathetic brown eyes. She was scarcely more than five feet tall and her eyes were level with the top button of his uniform. She said:

"Griff Evans, Tŷ Mawr!"

She led him into the parlour and they talked for a while in their native tongue. She told him her mother was upstairs in bed, a little better but still quite poorly. Her father was asleep in his surgery. He had been too unwell to see the evening patients; she had had to send them away. She took him upstairs to see her mother, who said he must stay the night. Mrs Jones insisted, in spite of her daughter's protests, that he should read a letter from the head-mistress of the school in Chester where Katie had been a boarder for several years.

My dear Mrs Jones,

I cannot resist the strong inclination I feel (though *very* busy) to slip a few words into Catherine's envelope to tell you how deeply we regret to part with her.

She has been a most pleasant, loving and attentive pupil. That she will be a great comfort to you both as a friend and companion, I cannot for a moment doubt. She has a mind capable of high cultivation, and were it not for an unusual amount of timidity, it would be known and acknowledged that her abilities were of a superior character. I expect she will prove in future life *no ordinary Christian*.

When he was a hundred years old, Griff wrote to a relative about the simple supper he had shared that night with Katie Jones.

She made no fuss. She told me she had no proper dinner for me but if I was hungry she would give me some food or else I must go to the village inn. I preferred staying with her and take what pot luck she might give, and she gave me a basin-ful of gruel with an egg beaten into it. I never relished food better than then. I had had a long journey and was hungry.

40

Next morning, Katie walked down the village with Griff to see him off on the coach. He asked if he might write to her, and she said she would be pleased if he would.

In December, having discovered that her birthday was on the 11th, he sent her a shoulder wrap "to keep you warm while you are sitting up with your mother at nights." For the first time in his life Griff was in love.

They exchanged letters into the spring of 1861 and then he went to see her again. As they sat on a log beside the river Banwy, he asked her to marry him. Katie, however, felt it was too soon for her to think of marriage. They had met several times when she was a child, she said, but they did not know each other. Even so, Griff pleaded, he would like to speak to her father about it, and then when she was a little older he might ask her again. But Dr Jones was not prepared to allow his seventeen year old daughter, just out of school, to become a soldier's wife. He told Griff that her parents needed her at home, and although he might write to her, marriage was out of the question for a long time.

In mid-June, Katie received a hastily-written note from Griff. He was to embark almost immediately for Canada and would have no chance to see her or his parents before he left. He added that he would probably be absent from Britain for several years. At this point she may well have decided that her brief romance with Griff, Tŷ Mawr, was ended.

CHAPTER FIVE

Aboard "The Great Eastern"

Before breakfast on Sunday, June 9, 1861, the Principal Veterinary Surgeon summoned Evans and, in his stiff, formal way, told him that as a matter of urgency the British Government was sending a force to Canada to deal with the Fenian risings. The force was to include the 4th Battery of the 4th Brigade, and he had been asked to name a veterinary surgeon to go with it. At the start of his Canadian diary, Griff wrote:

> He said to me: "You are the man."

Mr Wilkinson explained that the main part of the battery had already departed for "the Camp" (Aldershot) and would be leaving almost immediately for Canada. Griff saw no reason why he should not carry out the social programme he had planned for that Sunday, so:

> First to the Welsh Cymanfa, at Poplar, where I heard excellent sermons morning and afternoon. Went on to Greenwich and had tea with Stoneham.

Stoneham was an experienced soldier who advised Griff on the many problems which might arise when embarking a force of men and horses for overseas service. He mentioned that Smith, Griff's *bête noir*, had already left for the Camp.

> Went to Blackheath to meet Gardiner and had supper with his family. It was 11 p.m. when I returned to the barracks

42

and was told we were to march from Aldershot next Thursday.

So he had only one and a half days to prepare to leave Woolwich.

Monday June 10.
Went to the Royal Horse Infirmary early. Saw my cases. Made up my case books. Arranged for medicines to take with me to Canada. Afterwards reported myself to the Colonel who promised to obtain for me a provisional route to go to Aldershot from the General, as no order for it had come from the War Office. I did lots of other things and went to bid General Sir Richard Dacres goodbye. He told me he would not give me the route until he had been officially informed from the War Office that I was to go. . . .
They had no business to order an officer out of the garrison without informing him first. He would teach them that lesson. After I had represented the inconvenience I might be put to by delay, he ordered a telegram to the Horse Guards, asking whether I was to go to Canada.

The General, probably harassed by the emergency arrangements, was evidently not in the best of tempers that morning. However, Evans saw no reason why he should be involved in an argument over protocol and decided to settle the matter for himself. As he said in a letter to his father, "I was not going to be a pawn in their game".

As I wanted to go to London on other matters, I went direct to the War Office to expedite the business. The order was made in my presence and I was assured General Dacres would receive it in a few hours. I did business at many places in London and returned to Woolwich by 8 p.m. Wrote letters, made up and packed all papers, books, clothes etc which kept me busy till after midnight.
Tuesday June 11.
This morning I had to go for the forage and lodging allow-

ance for self and servant. No time to call on friends . . . I was in time for the noon train with my horse and groom, but my valet and baggage were one minute late, so they had to follow by the next train for Aldershot.

After all the rush, the 4th Battery did not, in fact, leave the Camp at Aldershot until Monday 17th. Griff welcomed the respite as he needed time to give the battery horses a thorough examination, to check the forage and medical supplies and the arrangements for the long march to Birmingham, whence the Battery was to proceed by train to Liverpool for embarkation.

By Sunday morning his tasks were complete and he took the day off for a pilgrimage to the old town of Farnham with which his father's hero, William Cobbett, had a lifelong association. Describing the visit to his father, Griff reminded him that Cobbett, too, had been a soldier in Canada.

Next day, he marched with the battery into Berkshire "at the pace of walking horses, about 3½ miles an hour." Each horse carried baggage not much more than the weight of an average man.

They reached Reading the first night and Abingdon on the next, and by Wednesday evening they were at Woodstock.

Picked up fossils along the way and found one excellent colite . . . About two miles from Oxford we came to the top of a hill where all at once we saw that city of palatial colleges and churches beneath . . . It reminded me of the Crusaders when they first came in view of Jerusalem . . . It was uncommonly hot.

At Woodstock, the officers were permitted to visit Blenheim, where Lord Randolph Churchill, father-to-be of Sir Winston Churchill, was at that time being prepared for Eton. Among all the magnificence of the art treasures and furnishings of the palace the one item Griff mentioned in his diary was an old teapot used by Oliver Cromwell:

It will hold about 1½ to 2 pints. A lion sits on the lid.

Next day, starting as usual between six and seven in the morning, the battery marched to Warwick and on Friday to Birmingham. Griff was exhilarated by the march and the responsibility resting on him for the battery's horses. He regretted that it was not always possible to billet them in healthy conditions.

I observed that the horses which had been billeted in close, badly-ventilated stables overnight perspired sooner and much more on the march next day than the horses billeted in freely-ventilated stables did. This was regular all along.

On Monday evening, after two days' rest, the battery, preceded by the band of the Irish Dragoons, marched through cheering crowds to the station. After Birmingham's warmth, Liverpool was a cold douche. The weather had changed and rain fell steadily as the troops arrived at four in the morning at Edge Hill station where they had to wait for six hours before marching through Liverpool to the landing stage. They were to board "The Great Eastern" which was anchored in mid-stream.

But the river was so rough that the drenched men and horses had to wait on the landing stage for several more hours until the gale abated. Meantime the horses had nothing to eat. At 3 o'clock the battery embarked by means of a steamboat from which the horses were hoisted one after the other to the deck of "The Great Eastern" where good stables had been prepared.

They spent three days rolling in the Mersey before the sea was calm enough for the great ship to weigh anchor. Meanwhile, immense crowds had gathered on both banks, and little ships loaded with spectators, followed her to the mouth of the river.

Griff had never been to sea before and he was fascinated by the ship:

"The Great Eastern" moves at the rate of $12\frac{1}{2}$ knots an hour and consumes 300 tons of coal daily. She is the largest and most wonderful ship ever built, for Noah's Ark is doubtful. She steers better at night because people are all below.

He filled pages of his diary with similar enthusiastic notes. Never before had it been possible in any ship to take horses out of their stables and exercise them.

But in this great ship every horse has an hour on deck to and fro. We have 100 horses of our battery and six horses of the officers of the 60th Rifles all exercised at once.

A week after leaving Liverpool he found that a horse had hydrothorax, and had to order it to be shot.

Early on July 1 he was astonished to see in mid-Atlantic what he took for mountains on the horizon. A sailor told him they were foghills: "I was reminded of what I had heard of Columbus' first voyage." In the afternoon the ship was enveloped in a thick fog, and a ship's officer said they had narrowly escaped running down a Cunard mail-ship, the "Arabia", returning from Boston. Later, they passed through a field of icebergs, "sliding between one that was ninety feet long, rising sixty feet above water, and another very huge one."

On the afternoon of July 4, Griff sighted the St Paul and Britton Islands; a couple of hours later they passed a three-masted ship, the American "Lizzie Southerd" of some 15,000 tons, "flying along in a favourable wind. Beautiful. I shall never forget it."

Early next morning, a pilot came aboard to take them up the St Lawrence River.

July 6.

Inhabitants all French. Thick forest except the clearings near the river. The French Canadians contrast wonderfully with the English or Scots Canadians in that they seldom extend their settlements far from the rivers by breaking into the forest inland. Steamers full of people, women and men sightseers, came down to meet us and shout the first cheers of welcome to us. The ships in harbour were densely crowded as also were all the quays, docks, stages, roofs and every possible place where people could stand to see us coming in slowly to our anchorage. The cheering was tremendous. Fireworks in the evening, and all the ships and houses specially lighted. We dropped anchor at 7 p.m. having made the quickest passage ever made. We would have been 24 hours sooner if we had not the fog and, with that, fear of icebergs.

I saw a greater number of pretty girls today than I did in the whole of our march in England.

But later, when he went ashore in Quebec, he did not think the girls so pretty.

I saw neither good-looking houses nor good-looking men nor pretty women, and I wondered where the girls came from to meet us coming up the river. Distance lends enchantment. The houses are roofed with tinned iron sheets cut out about the size and shape of Welsh slates.

The day after their arrival was a very hot Sunday; the troops had to remain on board and the Anglican chaplain, "a stickler for church regulations", held an open-air service, seeming to be unaware of the effect of the heat on the ranks.

July 7.
Chaplain Williams read the C.E. morning service on deck. All the Church of England men were paraded for it. He stood on the bridge in his clerical vestments and university degree bands, a soldier protecting him from the heat by holding an umbrella over his head. He read the whole service but did not preach. I stood on the bridge too and saw the effect. The men did not like it. Two of them fell out: slight sunstroke. All felt the heat too much.

Griff thought the service, lacking a sermon, was arid and pitied the men for having to attend. He felt compelled to make a protest:

47

I told the chaplain, before leaving the bridge, it would have been better to shorten the service by half and deliver a short, inspiring sermon as part of it. It was all gammon to read the prayers when the men did not join in. It was a mere formal mockery of religion. He replied that he thought it better to teach by the prayers of the church than by sermons.

Later, Mr Hammond, a Scottish revivalist, was given the colonel's permission to address the men. Mr Hammond's methods were much more to Griff's taste than Mr Williams':

His manner was suitable to the men, free and easy. They were all allowed to smoke when he addressed them. Several times in the course of his speech he sang popular airs to religious words in which the men joined heartily. After he left the deck the soldiers continued to sing hymns.

This irritated two infantry officers who ordered the men to stop singing and disperse. Angered, Griff strode up to the officers and said: "You have no right to interfere. The men can't say this to you, but I can. Let them sing if they want to!"

The battery disembarked the following Wednesday, and, after an overnight train journey "through primitive forest punctuated by wooden railway halts", they marched through Montreal to the old Cavalry barrack. The men were put under canvas and the officers in an empty house.

All of us could not get our baggage in last night. Major Penn and I had to sleep on the planked floor. We had our blankets and slept comfortably as soldiers should.

Next day he reported to Captain Waller, the Brigade Major.

Captain Waller took me for a drive round the Mount Royal,

from which there are beautiful views. He took me home to tea and I was pressed to remain the whole evening. Mrs Waller is good company and has an open mind. They gave me much useful information about this country and people.

At two o'clock next morning, officers and men were roused by the trumpet sounding the alarm, and they formed up with guns and harnessed the horses while the church bells rang in warning, but it was a false alarm, for nothing more than one of the wooden houses had caught fire. But a few days later the alarm sounded again, and this time it was indeed the Fenians.

As Evans prepared for his first taste of military action, a senior officer came to him and asked if he knew where Smith was. Griff, who some hours earlier had seen Smith entering a shabby house near the barrack, said that he would fetch him. He hurried to the house, which he suspected was a brothel, and clattered on the door and warned Smith that the battery was about to go into action and that he must report at once to Major Penn.

The Fenians were quickly routed and that was the last of that year's more serious incidents in Montreal.

Next day Smith called on Griff at his quarters.

He said he wanted to thank me for enabling him to avoid what might have been a serious charge. I was agreeably surprised by his change of heart. I invited him to take tea with me and it gave me great pleasure when he accepted.

CHAPTER SIX

The Body Snatchers

Evans found in Montreal that he had plenty of time on his hands, and characteristically determined to make good use of it. He approached the medical school at McGill University and persuaded them to accept him as a student.

He and his brother officers believed they were destined for a long stay; the British Government would hardly dispatch such powerful reinforcements to Canada merely to deal with a few rebels. The real danger must be that President Lincoln's Government, angered by Britain's sympathy for the South in the American Civil War, might seize on this as an excuse to invade Canada.

> I sought permission to study at McGill from my commanding officer. I explained that I should not let it interfere with my military duties. On this condition, and on the understanding that I might have to terminate my studies suddenly, he agreed, although he appeared to think it was incredible that I should want to be a doctor of medicine when I was already a veterinary surgeon.

Griff then sent off an unromantic and undiplomatic letter to Katie. After boasting that he was probably the first army officer ever to enrol as a medical student at McGill, he continued:

> The University was founded in 1811 and has a very good medical school. If the battery stays in Montreal for three years there is no reason why I should not be a doctor by 1864. A medical degree will be of great assistance in my career. I think it is right that I should make the most of my

opportunities and see what I can of the world. I shall always
think of you warmly but you must not consider yourself in
any way bound to me. I trust your parents are in better
health . . .

In reply to this well-intentioned but scarcely ardent letter, Katie
sent a cool little note wishing him success in his medical studies.

Griff had come a long way both intellectually and in strength of
character in the six years since he left the Veterinary College. He
had read extensively and his curiosity ranged over many fields.
He had gained more assurance and learned how to mix with his
fellow men. But he still had much to learn about women.

He now set himself a rigid routine. In the morning, wearing the
newly-redesigned Royal Artillery uniform for veterinary officers,* he kept meticulous watch on the horses in his charge and
the men who tended them. Then he changed into civilian clothes
and for the rest of the day became a student. He spent much of his
first year at McGill, as he later said, in cutting up corpses with
Gray's Anatomy in one hand and a scalpel in the other. The
students were expected to buy corpses for dissection with their
own money, and for this purpose the bodies of negro slaves were
smuggled in from America, packed in casks labelled as
"groceries". Officials tolerated this traffic which was known as the
"regular channel" for obtaining dissection material. But some
students, because of poverty or dare-devilry or because they
disliked putrefying flesh, preferred the "irregular channel"
which simply meant snatching bodies from their graves. Griff
himself insisted on obtaining bodies only from the acknowledged
source, which was a reasonably inexpensive method.

I could sometimes afford to have three at once so as to work
on different anatomical subjects the same evening.

Ever-inclined to attribute the world's evils to alcohol, he added:

*The uniform was blue with a white belt and a black pouch for instruments,
surmounted by the R.A. busby, with a red plume to distinguish the veterinary
calling. Evans rode a horse with the shabraque of the Royal Artillery.

Some of the students concerned (in stealing bodies) dared each other under the influence of drink, and then carried out their evil work so carelessly that they were sometimes caught and punished.

Griff established a real friendship with his anatomy lecturer, Dr Nelson, who was dedicated to medical research and more receptive to new ideas than most of his colleagues. With his veterinary knowledge and the elementary grounding in medicine he had received from Dr Pughe in Wales, Griff made rapid progress and Nelson treated him more as a colleague than as a student.

Dr Nelson was evidently well aware that some of his students were guilty of body-snatching, but like his namesake he turned a blind eye. He explained to Griff that the students of the French medical school made a scientific business of stealing bodies which they did for reasons of thrift and also because, in the icy grip of a Canadian winter, the bodies were well preserved and preferable to those smuggled in from America. He described the technique of these Catholic students who, he claimed, were so skilled that they were rarely detected. He told Griff that

> . . . they would go to a recent grave when it was snowing, and dig down to the coffin, place the lifted earth in as compact a heap as possible, cut the lid off with a proper instrument from head to middle, place a loop of cord round the neck of the corpse, pull it out of the coffin, replace the lid and lifted earth, cover all with snow. The descending snow will obliterate footmarks if the last of the party will sweep it about evenly. Carry the corpse to the provided sleigh - and off.

During the winter 1861/2 Griff was involved in two macabre incidents arising from body snatching which he describes in his Canadian diaries in his usual unemotional style, the restraint of his language enhancing the horror. At about the turn of the year some students had exhumed the body of a woman who, unknown to them, was closely related to two of their fellow students: she was the mother of one and the aunt of another.

52

I was dissecting when the fresh corpse of a white woman was placed on the table next to mine. Being white she was presumably exhumed. Presently a student came up to her, gazed, then exclaimed with horror: "Good God! That is my aunt! Her son is down at the chemical lecture and will be up here soon!"

He partly fainted and was supported by two others who led him out weeping. There was consternation as the students wondered what could be done. One of us said, "Dissect the skin off the face quickly." Agreed. Two students commenced doing so immediately, and fortunately did enough to make recognition impossible before her son came in. I watched him. He went to see the new white subject, cheerfully joked with the two dissectors, congratulated them on their successful venture, et cetera. He was often at the table afterwards during the course of the dissection.

Griff amplified his story some time later:

The nephew who recognised the body of his aunt disappeared for a long time, supposed to have sickened. He dared not tell his relatives of his discovery because he had been secretly implicated in the exhumation and dissection of another body. The students who had exhumed his aunt had no thought of her being related to anyone at the college. They were sincerely sorry to find she was so, and would have been glad not to proceed with dissecting her, if they could dispose of her otherwise without causing questions.

A few weeks later, on the evening of February 21, 1862, Evans was working alone in the dissecting room when Dr Nelson came in, obviously distressed.

"Mr Evans," he said, "I need your help".

He explained that a sleighman had reported to the police for reward that five students had recently exhumed two bodies, a man and a younger woman. The police had not yet recovered the bodies and had as yet identified only one of the students, so no charge had been made. But a lawyer representing the two families of the deceased had written to Nelson, because the identified student was a private one of his. The families were anxious to avoid publicity and so long as the bodies were returned to them *unmutilated* they were prepared to take no action. Nelson told Griff:

"This is where I need your help. The four other students have come forward and confessed to me they were involved, and are waiting to show me where they have hidden the bodies. I am most anxious that nobody should know of this affair, least of all the University authorities. Those bodies must be returned at once. I am asking you, as a senior and sensible student, to assist me in conveying them to a house some miles from here where the families are waiting, and to witness the necessary legal formalities. One of the students will have to drive the sleigh. Will you come?"

Without hesitation, Griff went with Dr Nelson.

The five students led them to a shed behind the College and showed them the bodies. Griff's matter-of-fact diary continues the story:

They lay naked on their backs, side by side, feet of one to head of the other, in a bed of soft snow. One an old man, the other a middle-aged woman. Both of course were frozen thoroughly hard, appearing quite fresh, no post-mortem changes. It was a beautiful clear moonlight. Dr Nelson got in beside one and I beside the other.

The students had thoughtfully provided old overcoats and hats, and they wrapped up the corpses and put the hats on their heads. Griff grasped the female corpse to keep it steady, and Dr Nelson the male one.

We pulled the buffalo robes well up so that if we passed through a crowd we should not be suspected of wrong. We arrived all right at the house appointed, and there delivered the bodies to the lawyer, and the relatives, who identified them and gave Dr Nelson the legal assurance promised not to prosecute the students, or to publish the name of any one

54

of them. Of course Dr Nelson expressed his own sincere regret.

Anyone less trusting than Griffith Evans might have wondered whether there had been, for some reason, a concerted attempt to hush up the incident. It was only later he realised the risk he had run. If he and Nelson had been caught conveying stolen bodies he might well have lost his commission and perhaps suffered even worse penalties. The governors of McGill later made a ruling – possibly on Dr Nelson's advice – that on pain of expulsion students must not bring corpses into the dissecting room unless they had been acquired in the authorised manner.

Griff's professor at McGill, Dr Campbell, drew his students' attention to the "new pathology" which was being championed by the Edinburgh scientist, Brunt. In its basic simplicity it confirmed Griff Evans' own beliefs, and he seized on it eagerly. A staunch believer in preventive medicine, Evans always held that nature intended all human organs to function with ease, and that any "dis-ease" must at once be remedied before other bodily functions became affected. Attention to nature's signals would avoid the onset of disease or would remedy it in its initial stages. He was possibly thinking of the tragic neglect of his ear trouble as a child when he wrote:

People should not tolerate malfunctioning in themselves or in their children, unless it is beyond repair.

Animals, if left to themselves, tend to observe and act on these signals more than humans, who are apt to aggravate disease by bad eating and drinking habits, bad breathing and lack of exercise.

If he had chosen to expound these views in his final thesis, Evans might have found his examiners more in sympathy than they proved to be for the subject he preferred – the pathology and history of tuberculosis, the killer of his generation. He submitted what we now recognise must have been a remarkably intelligent dissertation, but it was greeted with scepticism. He insisted that tuberculosis was an infectious illness; that consumptives should be isolated from healthy people, and their nurses should take special precautions; and, most important, that if sufferers were given enough fresh air and sunshine they might be cured.

In the eighteen-sixties Evans' fresh-air theories must have seemed nonsensical. This was long before scientists had grasped the idea of bacterial infection, and eighteen years before Robert Koch discovered the bacillus of tuberculosis. Everyone believed that consumptives must be kept in close, sealed bedrooms where no cold air or night "humours" could enter. True, most of them died, but they would surely die sooner, it was argued, if allowed to breathe cold air, especially night air, through an open window.

When "De Pathogenesi et Histologia Tuberculosis" by Griffith Evans came up in Convocation, it was decided that it merited a "challenge." It was customary to "challenge" a student who put forward a completely new theory. Dr Fraser, the chief examiner, gave Evans a gruelling interview and he defended his theories with tenacity; but it is doubtful if any member of the examining board took his views seriously. They were, after all, merely only conjectures. He could only list possible and probable causes and produce but one case history; yet his reasoning was based on his own observations in Wales where he had seen consumptives coughing up their lungs in airless little rooms. He recalled men who were afflicted after marrying consumptive girls, and wives who had succumbed after nursing their doomed husbands. But he had one supporter in his own profession, Dr Campbell, who supplied him with his one case history – one of the doctor's own male patients. The doctor had given this patient three years to live, at most, and had advised him to tidy up his affairs and make the best of what life was left to him. The patient's favourite sport was duck-shooting, and as he was a bachelor he very sensibly wound up his business and went off to face death in the open air environment he loved, camping out and shooting duck. He lived like this for five years, wondering when he was going to die, and feeling better than ever. At length, he returned to Montreal and presented himself to Dr Campbell, who told Evans:

"I could hardly believe my eyes. The man was cured, and the only trace I could find of his old complaint was a slight depression in the chest where the mischief had been."

The examiners may not have agreed with Evans' hypothesis,

but his presentation of his case was said to be masterly, and his confidence probably impressed them. They decided he had earned his M.D. In the early summer of 1864 he became Dr Griffith Evans. One of his boyhood ambitions was fulfilled, and although he eventually rose to the rank of Colonel, he always preferred to be called Dr Evans.

His thesis on tuberculosis failed to have even the slightest influence on his contemporaries. It was never published, and was stowed away with other students' theses and eventually destroyed. Doctors continued to shake their heads over tuberculosis victims; countless tombstones bore silent witness to the impotence of medicine; the great killer of the Victorian age was to take its toll for many years yet.

More than half a century after Evans' graduation, McGill University opened a section of their Osler Library, devoted to the life and works of Griffith Evans, and described him as "one of McGill's most distinguished sons."

CHAPTER 7

Colonial Canada

As a relaxation from his medical studies Griff occasionally went on long excursions into the backwoods. In his Canadian diary he tells how one such expedition led to his saving the life of a frostbitten man.

In the autumn after his arrival in Montreal, he and an Irish officer, Lieutenant Barton, while out on a frontier patrol had come across a remote log cabin on the shores of Lake Champlain; they discovered that the owners were fellow Celts, a family called Peters, who had been forced to emigrate from Scotland when their Highland croft was absorbed into a deer park. Griff and Barton were given a warm invitation to come and stay. Late in the following January, on a bitterly cold morning, the two young officers set off for the week-end. They crossed the St Lawrence river by an ice bridge where the force of the arrested current had tossed up blocks of ice four feet thick. Then they took a train to Lacolle, "about the size of Towyn", where the Peters' son met them with a sleigh.

Mrs Peters gave us a real Highland welcome . . . no affectation . . . entirely natural. They are proud of their cabin which they built themselves with logs sealed with clay, an American stove and stone fireplace designed to burn wood . . . Mr Peters said that the first Scottish settlers had only open chimneys, like those in the Highland crofts . . . During an excellent supper of fresh beef and pork I enquired the source of such tender meat in winter, and I was told that it was killed some months before. The joints were dipped in water which froze immediately and the meat was then packed in casks to be preserved as fresh as the day it was killed.

After supper Mrs Peters took out her pipe and puffed contentedly, and Mr Peters talked nostalgically of Scotland. He said that although they had more wordly goods in Canada, they never ceased to pine for their native land, and the older they grew the more their longing increased.

I asked how many pipes a day Mrs Peters smoked. She replied: "Oh dear me, I dinna know, whenever I feel uncomfortable or vexed I take my pipe and smoke it off. And if I am more happy than usual I smoke my pipe too. Sometimes I canna sleep in the night, and then I get out of bed and smoke a pipe. It is a great comfort but a verra *bod* habit."

Next day, the Peters' son took Griff and Barton on a sleigh tour of farmhouses along the boundary of New York State, and Griff bought "a splendid skin of a large dog fox for six shillings, well dressed and tanned, soft and warm." On their homeward journey, as they waited in Lacolle station for the evening train to Montreal, Griff and Barton discovered a French Canadian lying helpless on the platform. He was suffering from severe frostbite. As Barton spoke fluent French, the man was able to tell them his story.

He came from Montreal and had been on his way to visit relatives when nightfall overtook him and he sought shelter in a ruined house. Next morning, his hands and feet were swollen with frostbite. Local people had given him the common treatment:

The victim's limbs are covered with soft snow which melts gradually and thaws the limbs. They become blue and black, and are wrapped in flannel.

Then someone had sent for the Roman Catholic priest who had shrived the sick man. He gave him a letter of introduction to the Grey Nunnery Hospital – the Hotel Dieu at Montreal – and had him carried to the station.

He was left there for chance, without money or help. There was no-one available to take charge of him. Then I took charge of him.

I wrapped his limbs in my railway rug and put my comforter, the one Mother gave me, over his head. I had him carried into a first class compartment. It was evident he was suffering awfully, but he did not murmur a complaint.

About half way to Montreal, a Major of the 47th regiment came into the compartment with a dramatic story of how he had two days previously seen a smart horse and sleigh, with three men in it, sink out of sight in the river as a result of a sudden crack in the ice. This was not cheering news for Griff, who had to get his patient across the St Lawrence.

When we arrived at the Montreal terminus, the sleighman I hailed was good enough to say he would convey the frozen man and me to the hospital, and he would not allow me to pay him. It was a long sleigh, suitable for the patient to be lying down on a straw bed and wrapped in buffalo skins. The sleigh was shaken fearfully in crossing the St Lawrence river. We were upset once, but fortunately on my side, so the patient was not thrown out. The traces broke twice and the light of our lamp was extinguished. However we got on fairly well considering the state of the track.

Griff's prejudice against Roman Catholicism, heightened no doubt by the priest who had left the frostbitten man to fend for himself, is evident in his description of a nineteenth-century Canadian nunnery.

The Nunnery Hospital is a little out of the city. We arrived there about nine. I rang the big bell, pulled too hard, broke the bellrope. It is an immensely large building, nunnery and hospital included, recently built, enclosed by a great thick high wall like a prison, which it is for the nuns. We were for a long time knocking at the door before anyone opened it. I told the portress our business, she reported it to a Sister, who went and reported it to the Mother.

A favourable answer came to us, the great door was opened, we drove into the ante-court. The door was closed behind us with a great bang, bolted and locked.

I cannot forget what I saw and felt then, shut within this prison. Fronting me, a huge building, strong, solid, plain. No ornament but some images and a huge crucifix. It is night; moonless. The sky and stars are not so clear and bright as usual in Canada when it does not snow. Snow threatened. Mental gloom. Fronting me, a flight of 25 or 30 steps to a platform, where I see six or eight nuns, one of them holding a large lamp. They have on a grey gown, great big stiff white collars covering their shoulders. A white napkin tied round the head of each, like old women in Wales with a headache. Each has a black hood, and plaid apron pockets. A large crucifix hangs from the neck down to the apron.

I was invited up to the platform.

There I told them all I knew and heard of the patient, emphasising he had a letter of introduction from the priest who shrived him. They expressed their sympathy.

There were two or three particularly good-looking girls among them, pure and sweet countenance, good manner of speaking, freely and heartily in English. I wished they were somewhere else, and thought I would willingly risk my life to help them out of that prison to freedom if they wished.

I helped them to undress the patient in a large, clean, well-ventilated ward. I felt gladly relieved in leaving him in the tender care of the nuns . . . In driving to my quarters I thought of the Dark Ages . . .

30 January.

Visited the patient at the Hotel Dieu. He was glad to see me and is improving.

The French Canadian survived, but only after amputations. Griff records that he had been given alcohol by the local people in the village where he sought shelter, and elsewhere in his diaries he rails at the popular belief that alcohol was beneficial in preventing frostbite:

During my first winter in Canada, Royal Artillery sentries

on night duty were given the usual allowance of rum in the mistaken idea that it would help them to resist the cold. But so many sentries were found asleep and frozen on duty that the medical officers supported my suggestion that hot, strong coffee be substituted for rum. After that, no sentry in the regiment was ever found frozen at his post. I was often out when the thermometer was 42 degrees below zero. I attributed my immunity to frostbite to the fact that I was a teetotaller with a good circulation. I also took the simple precaution of rubbing my face with the back of my mittens, both when going out from warm to cold, and when coming in from cold to warm.

Smug about his own good health, Griff seems almost callous about the fate of a Canadian guide who died of exposure on a sleigh trip during another leave excursion.

Accompanied by his friend, Captain Waller, Evans set off with a driver-guide on a fifty-mile trip to Huntingdon, then an outback village. But when they reached a hamlet called Allen's Corner, the guide said they could go no further. Griff had walked beside the pony to help it, but even so the animal was exhausted. Determined to press on "at least as far as the village of Durham for the night", they found another sleigh and two guides, one to drive and one to walk in front. Once more they set off, Waller tucked in rugs in the sleigh "because he was a married man", and Griff running or walking behind on the ice-track on the river. Conditions became more gruelling and the guides warned that to go on would be dangerous. But Griff, exhilarated and light-hearted, tossed caution to the winds, and his diary has cheerful little ink drawings with captions like "Here we are, thrown into the snow when the sleigh upsets." His mood astonished the two French guides, who "could not understand our fun", which was not surprising as they had missed the ice-track. One of them was bewailing this fact, "his voice as if he wept".

Eventually, at midnight, they did reach the little hotel at Durham. Griff's frozen trousers "stood up by themselves like two glass cylinders in front of the stove until they melted", while he rubbed himself all over with flannel, drank hot milk and ate eggs and bread and butter. He and Waller were none the worse, but one of the guides, a Mr Sainte-Marie, was so chilled by exposure that he never recovered. When Griff heard, some days later, of the poor man's death, he wrote:

I am sorry. I think it was his fault in keeping in the sleigh after wetting his feet and legs, instead of exercising them as I did.

And then, with a slightly defiant tone:

We did give the guide more dollars than he asked for.

In the summer of 1863, Griff determined to seek out a tribe of Red Indians and live with them for a few days. He applied for a week's leave and sought a companion among his fellow officers, but because of the hostility between white man and Indian in America, he could find nobody with any wish to join him in his frontier adventure.

James Meyrick was then serving with the 4th Brigade in another sector, and Griff wrote, inviting his old friend to apply for leave and go with him. Meyrick's reply was to send a cutting from a newspaper dated December 26, 1862, which described the recent American revenge on the Sioux. It was illustrated by a horrific drawing captioned "Execution of the Thirty-Six Sioux Indians". This was a branch of the Sioux that Griff hoped to discover; he had heard there were some of them ranging between the Red River and Minnesota. Meyrick warned him that he could hardly expect the Sioux to tolerate a white man in their midst. He asked if Griff were aware that in Minnesota there was a State reward for an Indian scalp? Any reasonably intelligent Red Indian, seeing Griff prowling around, would come to only one conclusion: that he was hunting for scalps to collect the reward.

Griff pasted the picture of the thirty-six hanged Indians into his scrapbook and wrote back to Meyrick that he would go alone.

I am informed that the stationmaster at Milwaukee has ways of getting in touch with Indians who travel from there to New York to take part in Barnum's Circus. I shall pay one of these to guide me to an Indian settlement. They will see I am unarmed and they will trust me. I have been advised to travel looking obviously Canadian so that I am not mistaken for an American, and to take with me some tobacco from the Red River area. I have arranged for some to be sent to me, and I shall wear Canadian shoes with square toes.

He made the journey of almost a thousand miles by fast train which stopped only to take in wood and water. Milwaukee, on the west shore of Lake Michigan, was in those days a developing port. It now seems unimaginable that a stationmaster at Milwaukee should "walk to the end of the platform and whistle up a couple of Red Indians from the woods". Yet that, it seems, is exactly what that official did for Griff in the early summer of 1863.

He started a peculiar whistling. After some time, two Red Indians emerged from the woods and came towards us.

The Indians, who had picked up a little English in Barnum's Circus, agreed to guide Griff into the forest and find some Indians for him to meet. The stationmaster had a few horses for hire, and Griff hired two, one for himself and one between the Indians, as he had reckoned on paying for only one guide.

He left a suitcase of clothes with the stationmaster, for he hoped to see something of Milwaukee on the way back.

As they rode into the forest, which was fifty miles across and two hundred miles long, the guide whose turn it was to run alongside chattered in pidgin English he had learned in New York.

He kept repeating five words: Jesus, God, Church, Devil and Damn.

They rode straight across the woods, but in all the fifty miles they did not come across a single brave. They emerged in a village on the other side, and there on the fence of the very first house hung a row of scalps drying in the sun. Griff reined in his horse. The guides explained that these were scalps of Indians murdered by the householder for the State reward. They looked around uneasily.

We stayed only to replenish our water bottles, and I undertook to see that no white man caused them any trouble. We plunged back into the forest, and, at last, after sleeping beside the ponies until dawn, we came upon a settlement of Indians in a clearing. The women were squatting on the ground, listening to a boy playing the flute.

The guides went ahead and beckoned to me to follow. As I rode nearer I saw that the boy was European. The guides said that he had been stolen as a baby and brought up as a male Indian. It began to thunder. There was no sign of any male Indian. Here they were all squaws except the boy. The men were out hunting until evening.

I was taken to an empty wigwam and left there alone. I sat down on the ground and said to myself "Well, at least I can say I have sat in a wigwam, although there is nobody for me to talk to." But soon, a number of young women came silently in and, without a word, they rustled down into a semi-circle, squatting with their backs to my back, supporting me like an arm-chair. They made it clear I was to lean against them, and make myself rested and comfortable. I thought that this was superb hospitality, and wished my brother officers could see me now as I reclined against their pretty brown shoulders. The girls stayed until the thunderstorm was over. Then they stole away as silently as they had come.

Griff stayed on in the wigwam lest he offended his hostesses by emerging, and at dusk one of the guides came to tell him that the braves had returned from hunting, and the chief wished to see him. He was led to the chief's wigwam to pay his respects.

I was entertained and fed, the guides acting as interpreters. I greatly admired some wooden spoons and bought some to take home. I tried to explain that in my country, young Welshmen carved spoons for the girls of their choice and called them love-spoons. The evening was a great success. I

65

told them about Wales and spoke a little in Welsh and they seemed to be interested.

In the early morning, after a good sleep under some furs, he moved about amongst the squaws who were cooking breakfast, and admired their children. He had always been fond of the young of any species, and he was particularly taken with a tiny baby, a "papoose", asleep in a papoose-carrier slung from the branch of a tree.

When I took my leave, the guides told me that the tribe was willing to sell me a papoose-carrier to take home, as I seemed to admire it so much. I explained that I was really admiring the baby, but I should like to buy the carrier.

Amidst courteous farewells, he rode away into the forest with his two Indian guides, his papoose-carrier, and the spoons.

Back at Milwaukee railway station, he returned the ponies, paid the guides, collected his suitcase, changed, and once again became a well-dressed young British officer in mufti.

He had been given the address of a young Welsh girl born in Towyn, who was now living near Milwaukee. The girl offered to take him on a tour of the port, and when they came to a photographer's at No 16 Wisconsin Street, they agreed as two natives of Towyn that it would be a good idea to be photographed together and send the likenesses home to their respective relatives. In due course, Griff sent the photograph home to his mother. It shows him to be a debonair young man wearing a velvet collared casual jacket and light trousers, his fair hair neatly parted and his whiskers well-trimmed as befitted an army officer. He was leaning on the arm of a chair in which sat a demure, plain girl, her hands encased in net gloves. Griff saw nothing amiss in being photographed with another man's fiancée almost on the eve of her wedding.

The picture, however, was to cause the kind of misunderstanding often described in romantic novels. Almost a year later, while she was staying at Gwalia Villa in Towyn with her aunt, Miss Catherine Jones, Katie visited Tŷ Mawr. Propped up on the dresser amongst other pictures she saw this photograph of Griff leaning intimately over the seated girl.

A few months afterwards she heard from her aunt in Towyn that Griff Tŷ Mawr had qualified as a doctor. She wrote him a formal note of congratulation. And when Griff wrote to thank her, and then wrote again, she did not answer. The photograph had convinced her that she should put him out of her mind and heart.

When Griff's letters were ignored, he wrote no more.

CHAPTER EIGHT

An Interview with Abraham Lincoln

In the third week of June, 1864, Veterinary Officer Evans set off from Montreal, hoping to reach the Federal lines of the American Civil War. He had been given six weeks' convalescent leave to recover from a bad bout of dysentery. He wanted to study conditions in field hospitals.

By this time it had become almost impossible for a British officer to obtain a permit to enter the Northern lines. General Lindsay, commanding the British Army in Canada, and Dr Muir, the Director of Hospitals, had both failed to obtain passes. This was hardly surprising as British sympathies were with the South, and it was well known that English firms were supplying munitions to General Lee's army.

Evans' plan had been greeted with derision by his fellow officers and with strong protest by the medical officer who had attended him in his illness. A long journey to Washington, even if he got no further, was no way to spend his sick leave.

Nevertheless, he sought the permission of his commanding officer to make the trip, arguing that to visit front-line hospitals would be an invaluable help in extending his medical knowledge, and, to everyone's surprise, the CO agreed. He was doubtless convinced that young Evans would not get very far, but he said there was no harm in his trying.

The omens for his project could scarcely have been less propitious. For the North it was one of the gloomiest periods of the three-year-old war. Ulysses S Grant, newly-appointed chief general of the Federalist forces, had launched the terrible Battle of the Wilderness, resulting in a degree of human slaughter that was to shock the world.* The Federalists were now digging in, hoping to defeat the South by a brutal process of attrition. President

* Grant lost 60,000 men in this campaign; the Confederates lost 40,000. America lost more men in this "war of brothers" than in the whole of the Second World War.

Lincoln had no lack of problems, and, in addition to everything else, he had to concern himself with a campaign for the Presidential election.

But, as usual, Evans had made careful preparations. He approached a number of distinguished men at McGill University who provided him with introductions to some potentially useful Americans, including the eminent scientist, Professor Joseph Henry, a close friend of President Lincoln. He was also given a letter to Lord Lyons, the British Ambassador in Washington. He said forthrightly that he intended to wear his British uniform throughout. There was to be no deceit. (A young officer in his brigade had just been sent home ignominiously after trying to smuggle himself into the Federal lines disguised as a Yankee soldier).

He went first to New York with an introduction to Dr Flint. The doctor's heart was doubtless warmed by Evans' keen interest in a binaural stethoscope which Flint had invented. Dr Flint, a man of considerable repute, numbered among his friends several notable medical men in the Federal armies, and, more important, no less personages than General Grant, General Meade, and General Thomas. To the delight of Evans, he wrote letters of introduction to all of them.

Arriving in Washington, where "I passed the Capitol, a splendid Grecian building, well worth coming from Montreal to see", Evans at once presented his letter of introduction to the British Ambassador. Lord Lyons, who was showing signs of overwork and worry, invited him to dine at the Embassy that evening, but regretted that he could do little to help him. He said he had recently been unable to help the General commanding the British Army in Canada or the Director General of Hospitals there, and, in his view, official passes were now impossible to obtain.

This was no news to Evans, who then made his way to the Smithsonian Institute to see Professor Henry. Joseph Henry, a distinguished pioneer in electrical science, read his letter of introduction and invited him back to his house. The Professor's wife and daughter entertained him to tea and "asked me to make myself freely at home with them during my stay in Washington and to call at any time". After tea, the Professor said he would escort Evans to the White House the next day, and introduce him to President Lincoln personally "as soon as it could be arranged".

All of this must have been far beyond Lieutenant Evans' expectations, and his spirits were high as he went back to the Embassy for his dinner appointment. Lord Lyons was much impressed by the Professor's promise to take Evans to the White House.

> He entertained me very hospitably, taking my hand in both his when I left and giving it a good shaking. He looks a kind, good-natured, middle-aged man.

The British Ambassador had an unenviable task. He was trying to maintain reasonably cordial relations with the White House while Britain was continually being accused of partisanship towards the South. He was also concerned in guarding the interests of a great number of British nationals in America, many of them recent immigrants. During dinner, the Ambassador showed how heavily this problem weighed on his mind. Every day, he said, cases of kidnapping of British subjects for service in the Northern army were reported to the Embassy. In his diary account of the conversation, Evans wrote:

> A short time ago, seven Irishmen were kidnapped from the same place, two are still missing, four are known to have been killed in the late engagements and one remains wounded.
> The usual mode is for the press-gang to drug the man's food or drink so that he loses consciousness. He recovers in a distant place to find himself dressed in Union uniform with some money in his pocket which he is told is part of his bounty.
> All the Embassy can do is to request the War Department to investigate the case, to give it a fair trial and report. None of those relieved get any compensation for there is no fund voted by Congress to meet such contingency.
> I enquired about Richard Hall of Montreal. His poor mother was very anxious about him when I last saw her. I am told he made a fool of himself by trading with the Southerners and has been fined and imprisoned until the fine is paid.
> Lord Lyons assures me that the Federals have lost nearly one hundred thousand men since the first of May last. No less than ten thousand were killed in eight days during the

At the age of 36, Griffith Evans, newly married, was looking "much better fed".

"The Great Eastern" in which Griff sailed to Canada in charge of more than 100 horses. "The most wonderful ship ever built".

Abraham Lincoln.

General Meade.

General Butler.

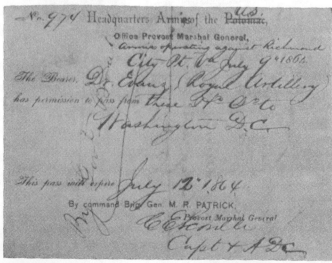

A pass issued to Lieutenant Evans during his tour of the American Civil War battlefields.

late fighting in the Wilderness. There are fifteen thousand sick and wounded in the city hospitals now. About sixty are buried daily.

One of Evans' fellow guests at the Embassy dinner was General Ramsay, who

... invited me to a party at his house after I left Lord Lyons, but I was too tired to accept his invitation. I asked the General what troops they had to garrison Washington, and he replied, "Only the invalids". He added: "Washington is one great hospital." I asked whether he thought it safe to leave it so unprotected and he said it was, for if an attack were made they would know in time to get troops from the front, for they expected more fighting every day and the army was much weakened and depressed by the late engagements and heavy losses, but ...*

Professor Henry took Evans to the White House on the following morning (June 24). Evans later provided three accounts of his interview with the President. The first was given to a reporter from "The Manchester Guardian".

Professor Henry was told to bring me to the White House at 10 a.m. After a formal introduction I told Mr Lincoln of my wish to visit the front. After a general conversation the President said he would talk about me to the military authorities and asked me to call again the next morning. When I called the second time, Mr Lincoln, whom I saw in his private room, said he would grant me a roving commission to visit the Northern army, and that he would direct all military authorities in the field to help me to go where I wished. But it was on one condition: that I was to make myself medically useful to the troops and help the wounded. I readily agreed.

*The rest of this passage is missing from Evans' diary. A number of pages have been torn out. They include his description of his meetings with President Lincoln and General Ulysses S Grant. It is believed these pages were stolen many years later by one of the several journalists who examined the diaries when interviewing Dr Evans.

In late life Dr Evans dictated to his daughter Erie some further memories of his meetings with Lincoln; he said that for the first interview Professor Henry and he were given precedence over a number of people waiting to see the President and were in Mr Lincoln's presence for half an hour.

I explained to Lincoln my purpose as a recently-qualified medical student to see all I could of medical work in the field and how Lord Lyons could not help me on account of anti-British feeling.

Lincoln looked at me and said, in effect: "You ought not to be surprised at our feeling, considering we have good reason to believe that British manufacturers are supplying our enemies with ammunition, and the British Government is not as careful as it should be as a neutral."

I said that although I was a British officer in uniform, I was not there to represent the British Government; and, although my personal sympathy was with the South because I thought they were putting up a good fight for their freedom, yet I was there simply as a recently-qualified medical student, wishing to see all I could, and to be free to follow my own line of observation. I said that armament makers were out simply to make money, and that if they could make as much by selling to Lincoln they would do so. I said that business men in the Northern states would be equally ready to make money by selling to countries at war in which America was neutral.

"At least," drawled Lincoln, "you are asking only to visit the field hospitals. You don't expect as much as the gentleman who asked for a pass through the Federal lines because he wanted to go to Richmond. I told him that within the past few years I have given passes to 100,000 men and not one of them has got there yet!"

He told me to return next day. In that second interview, Lincoln gave me a permit signed by the Quartermaster General granting me every facility to go wherever I wished, on condition I rendered medical help if called upon. He added that he would be obliged if I would call upon him on my way back through Washington to make a report. This I said I would be honoured to do.

The Quartermaster General who signed Evans' pass was General George Ramsay who had talked to him with so much frankness two days earlier at Lord Lyons' dinner party. Evans evidently had made a favourable impression on Ramsay who probably influenced the President's decision.

The third of Evans' recorded descriptions of his encounter with Lincoln was given to Dr Edgar de Witt Jones of the "Detroit News" who in 1935 went to North Wales to see "the last man alive in Britain who had met Abraham Lincoln". De Witt Jones, who said he "had been on the Lincoln trail for 25 years", wanted Evans' general impressions of the President. Dr Evans recalled:

Lincoln was a big man physically, big frame and loose-jointed, and when he crossed his legs his knees made a sort of mountain peak. . . . I knew I was in the presence of a great man. His simplicity impressed me from the first. He was direct and natural. There was nothing formal or stiff about him. He welcomed me cordially and I felt at ease in his presence.

I think my youth appealed to him. His face in repose was deeply sad but he smiled occasionally, and he chuckled once, I recall. Still, I wouldn't say he was jovial. Nor was he hurried, though many were waiting to see him. He was terribly burdened, you know . . . He had many characteristics, but there was nothing singular in him. He was a unity. He appeared to be kind, gentle, patient, considerate and, I would say, easy to get along with. Still, I can believe he had a will that nobody could break when he knew he was right. I thought him capable of anger yet holding it well in hand. He gave me no reason to believe him vindictive.

In the White House I saw a young man who was pointed out to me as Lincoln's son. I did not meet the youth. He looked to be in his twenties.*

When Lieutenant Evans reported his success to the British Ambassador, Lord Lyons was as pleased as he was surprised. He evidently felt that Evans had served a useful diplomatic purpose, and to show his approval he invited Evans once more to dine at the Embassy.

*De Witt Jones made a footnote to this: "Evidently this was not Tad but Robert."

His fellow guests at dinner that night expressed great interest in Evans' success at the White House. One of the American guests said that somebody had asked Lincoln why he had given this young doctor a pass when he had refused one to the Principal Medical Officer of the British Army in Canada, and that the President had replied: "Evans seemed like an honest man."

After dinner, three naval officers approached Evans and offered to accompany him on the first stage of his journey down the James River by river-steamer as far as Hampton Roads, where they were to join their frigate "Phaeton". He met them as arranged the following day (Sunday, June 26) and set off on his adventure.

His meeting with the naval officers proved to be most fortuitous. On the river steamer towards evening, he had a recurrence of dysentery, and asked to be put ashore at Fort Monroe, so that he could be taken to the field hospital there. But the officers protested that camp dysentery was very bad on shore, and it was unlikely he would receive proper attention. They insisted on taking him with them to "Phaeton", where he would be attended by the ship's surgeon.

Dysentery was rife in both Northern and Southern armies and many were dying of it. Evans believed that but for the hospitality and care of the British Navy he, too, might have died. He spent the better part of a week in "Phaeton".

The ship's officers were very friendly, and, like the army officers in Montreal, they were astonished at Evans' insistence on wearing British uniform for his venture. They urged him to wear the undress uniform of a Northern officer, which they said they could procure for him. But he declared that if he reached the front lines it would be as a British officer.

On June 29 he resumed his diary:

Commanding officers in the Navy have despotic power, but it is more limited than it was. One of the lieutenants tells me that since he entered the service in 1845 he has seen a midshipman flogged and another kept in irons for 48 hours without trial for outstaying his leave for four hours. One captain he served under used to inspect the polished tins and coppers with a new white kid glove on, and if it was soiled by any of the articles, the man who passed it as clean was put in irons and severely punished. Now, however, no-one except in extreme cases can be flogged within 24 hours after the crime, and not except by order of a court-martial.

HMS "Phaeton" was anchored near Fort Monroe, and when the surgeon allowed him to leave the ship for a few hours Evans presented himself at the gate and asked to see General Butler. The General sent back word that he wished to see his card and to know the purpose of his visit. Evans explained to the messenger that he was on the way to the front with a permit from President Lincoln and would like to visit the Fort hospital. Butler then provided him with an officer as a guide. Evans made copious notes on everything he was shown, and at the end of a very thorough inspection he told the guide that he thought the General should be given the chance to see what he had written before he took his notes away. The officer said he did not think the General wished to see him, but Evans persisted, and eventually he was summoned into Butler's presence.

General Benjamin Franklin Butler, by profession a criminal lawyer, who has been described as a careerist chameleon "sleepy-eyed with cunning", gave Evans a friendly greeting. He even produced maps and explained the position of the armies, and then invited him to come with him to the front next day as his guest. He actually offered to reserve for his use the tent which Mrs Butler had just vacated. Evans was to be at the departure point of the General's river steamer the following morning.

Butler, who had an above-average experience both of honest men and of scoundrels, was clearly impressed by Evans who, at 28, must have been a worthy representative of the British army, slim, upright, and with a confident air, cutting a dashing figure in uniform, as if he were just about to go on parade.

Next morning the ship's surgeon in "Phaeton" reluctantly agreed to Evans' departure, accepting that the General's invitation was a chance not to be missed.

The steamer was alongside the quay, but there was no sign of General Butler at the appointed hour, so Evans sat on his baggage and waited. Eventually, with a flourish of trumpets, the procession approached from the Fort. Evans stood at the salute, but to his amazement the General and his entourage ignored him and boarded the steamer as if he were not there. It was, plainly, a calculated snub. The gangway was pulled up and the vessel began to move.

Evans stood nonplussed. Then his natural determination asserted itself. He seized his baggage and threw it on board, leapt after the moving steamer, grabbing the gunwale and hanging on.

Owing to weakness from my recent illness, I narrowly missed falling into the river. I was left suspended for a time but I managed to climb aboard. I was determined to find out what was the matter. I came to the conclusion that some evil report had been spread about me. The same aloofness was shown when I got to the deck. No one took any notice of me. The officers passed me without a glance. That made me more determined than ever to find out what was wrong.

He sat doggedly on deck on his roll of blankets and waited for something to happen. At last it did.

An officer came up and said "You are Dr Evans?" I replied that I was. He said the General would receive me. I was taken to the General's cabin and found him lounging in a chair. I saluted and was kept standing during the following dialogue:
Butler: I suppose you were surprised by what happened this morning?
Evans: I was. Very much so.
Butler: I did not think you would follow me.
Evans: But you invited me to accompany you, Sir.
Butler: Last night we captured some mail from the South, intended for England. It included a dispatch from "The Times" correspondent. You can read it for yourself.
Then he threw the dispatch at me and almost threw a chair after it.

Evans read the dispatch. It included a private letter to the editor of "The Times" which referred frequently to "Beast" Butler. The General continued:

"That shows the sort of feeling in your country. Always in

favour of the South. It makes us mad. Do you expect me or my officers to hide our feelings about Englishmen?"

Evans replied that he was a Welshman and that he would not hide his feelings either. He replied:

"The South fight well and they are entitled to our admiration. In any event, Sir, I am here as your guest."

A slow smile spread over the chameleon general's face. From that moment his attitude changed, and he resumed the friendly treatment of the previous day. For the rest of the journey he was the perfect host.

Evans was always ready to defend Butler against criticism. To the end of his days, when the subject was raised, he would say, "Butler was *not* a beast!"*

Sunday, July 3, 1864. With General Butler's Army.
When I got ashore after the steamer journey, I was provided with a marquee, a servant, and the use of General Butler's car. He told me to stay as long as I liked. Got up at sunrise . . . Dr Woodhull rode out with me again to see the Front Line . . . General Butler is to the right of General Sherman, and his line extends for about two miles across the peninsula, between the two Appotomax rivers . . . He has cut down a belt of timber in front of his line, about 200 yards wide, which makes a very good protection . . . There are pickets posted here and there along the belt to watch the enemy, who are not far off, and these outposts are only relieved at night, for their only protection is darkness. They lie on the ground all day.

---

*When General Butler captured and became Military Governor of New Orleans in 1862, he became known as "Beast" Butler. This originated from a proclamation intended to stop high society girls from taunting the Yankee officers and spitting on the Union flag. Butler ordered that any lady found guilty of such insults must be treated as "an ordinary woman" and possibly jailed.

Immediately in the rear of this belt, a wall of earth and timber has been made, five feet high and six feet thick, zig-zag, with sandbags on top and small openings between the bags here and there to fire through . . .

There is a battery along this line of four or five guns every two or three hundred yards. The Regiment is encamped in the wood in the rear, and earthworks have been thrown up in front of the tents to protect them against splinters or shells. There are at present about 20,000 men in camp. The position is very strong, and 5,000 are supposed to be sufficient to hold it. At one place, the weakest part, where there is no forest in front, a narrow gap, we saw the advanced lines of the enemy, and their earthworks. The two lines are only about 100 yards apart here, and the advanced pickets of both sides are able to converse with each other.

After breakfast I visited the hospitals on this and the other side of the Appotomax River, also the hospital boat, which was full of patients ready to go to Hampton Hospital. All serious cases are conveyed down the river as soon as possible. I am much pleased with the sanitary condition of the army as far as I have seen it, and all the medical men seem to give special attention to the subject. I saw one surgeon who converts all gunshot wounds of the chest into incised wounds as soon as possible, and brings the lips together with silver sutures; then he hermetically seals the wound with collodion. Fluid always accumulates in the chest which is drawn or sucked through a bag attached to a peculiar cannula. I saw him operate, and he tells me that he is more successful than everybody else. But I doubt him.

Coloured soldiers are less liable to malaria and more subject to severe pneumonia (which is very fatal to them) than white soldiers.

It was very remarkable again to-day how quiet and noiseless all the white troops are, but a regiment of negroes that we saw encamped were as happy as princes, laughing and playing like children.

I went to the woods in the rear of the camp towards evening to collect beetles, but saw very few.

I am told that there are on average ten men a day deserting from the Confederates to the Federals, but I doubt it. Negroes, I am told, fight well in a charge, but not in a skirmish or when they have in any way to depend upon themselves.

There has been no firing on either side along this line since I arrived, but I hear an occasional report of the big guns across the Appotomax in the direction of Petersburg. I saw the spires of the churches of Petersburg very plainly this evening but it was too hazy to see Richmond.

A few days ago a "cavalry raid" was made to break up the railways leading to Petersburg, to cut off the supplies from the South. On their return they were accompanied by a large number of runaway slaves, men, women and children, who took advantage of their protection to come north and get free. The Confederates, however, attacked and killed a large number of the Cavalry, and sabred the poor slaves left and right, so few of them succeeded in escaping. One of them called on Dr McCormick and offered himself as cook, and was so engaged. I enquired of him about his past history. He is an intelligent-looking man, and says that before the war he was one of about seventy negroes, the slaves of a farmer ten miles from Richmond, who had reared him. When his master joined the Southern army he took him as a servant with him, and he was for some time past cooking for several officers, who messed together. I asked what he cooked for them, and he said "Crackers or bread, when we could get it, with bacon and sometimes potatoes. We made coffee of dried baked grain".

He said that the men were tired of the war, and the women and children were starving in Richmond.

CHAPTER NINE

Through the Federal Lines

On the following morning – it was Independence Day – Evans
decided to leave Butler's HQ and travel through the Federal lines
to the extreme Western sector commanded by General Meade,
where he hoped to witness an expected attack.

Monday, July 4
No demonstration here to commemorate the Independence. It was reported this morning that the enemy had
removed from his lines and the direction he took was
unknown. Scouts were sent out who returned to say it was a
false report. Dr McCormick tells me that the advanced pickets often give notice to each other when they are going to
fire, and that a kind of friendly feeling springs up between
them which has to be guarded against.
About 8.30 I bade adieu to General Butler. Doctors
McCormick and Derby accompanied me to the Bermuda
Hundred to show me the Medical Purveyor's department,
which is kept in a large boat there on the James River. It was
well supplied with medical comforts and luxuries. The
ordinary ferry having left, a special steamer was ordered to
take me to City Point . . .

At City Point Evans went straight to Dr Dalton and asked for his
help in getting down the lines.

Dr Dalton lent me a horse and mounted orderly to go to the
Provost Marshall's office for a pass to the HQ of General
Meade. Then I called on Brigadier General Ingolls, the
chief Quartermaster, with an introduction . . . He was

exceedingly kind and said he would be very happy to do anything he could for me. I told him how I was recovering from my late illness, and that I was anxious to proceed to the farthest end of the line in front as soon as possible so that I might work my way back as time and health would enable me. He said there were about fourteen miles to General Meade's HQ and that there was no regular conveyance. When I told him I was too weak yet for a long ride, especially as the sun was very strong, he ordered a covered carriage drawn by four splendid mules. A mounted orderly stood at the door ready for me.

I shall not soon forget that drive. The day was boiling hot with no wind, but owing to the constant movement of troops and all sorts of waggons and carts with stores, ambulance et cetera, the road was choking with dust. The road was simply a track made recently across country for the convenience of the army. The old roads, if they did not happen to be in the shortest direction, were discarded, fences pulled down for fuel, the crops in the fields trodden down, houses deserted or occupied by troops, or burnt down; thousands of recent graves of men killed or dead lately, and those so shallow that the stench from them was in places intolerable. Dead cattle and horses, men's accoutrements strewn about; it was indescribable and the effect was sad and sickening.

I arrived at the headquarters before 5 p.m., took my pass to Dr McFarley, the PMO, who gave me a letter to Dr Doghearty of the 2nd Army Corps. I called also on General Humphries* with introduction from Professor Henry. He introduced me to General Meade. I like them both very much, they are West Pointers, as the Volunteer officers call them. It is not difficult to tell a West Pointer from the others. All that I have seen have the manners of gentlemen.

Evans had been told that if General Meade were not actually engaged upon fighting, he would be found reading the Bible. And sure enough, he was sitting outside his tent in the evening cool, Bible in hand. Evans told the General what he had heard of him, and Meade replied, "Yes, it is the best book I have."

*Sic. General A.A. Humphreys, author of "Virginia Campaign."

81

Concluding the July 4 entry in his diary that night, Evans wrote:

In passing today through the many camps on my road from one end of the line to the other, the quiet was remarkable. Is that a calm before a storm? Fighting is expected again any day. It is certainly a calm after a series of very severe storms. Everybody looks sober and sad, few smile and then only a slight wave of expression on the surface of the mind. Officers and men talk in a subdued tone, and when asked they speak of "fearful slaughtering" of men that they were recently engaged in as if they wished to forget it. And they heartily long for their field duties to be over. This is the great National Day, but the only demonstration was the firing of a salute at noon, which no-one seemed to heed, and the dressing of the boats at the City Point.

July 5.

Later in the evening yesterday I heard a little cheering and shouting in the camp but it was only for a few moments. I was tired and went to sleep about 9 p.m. An engagement being expected almost ány hour, the camp had been cleared of all baggage et cetera not absolutely required. Dr Doghearty and the assistant surgeon had only one small bell tent between them. They had constructed a rude bedstead of branches of trees on each side of the tent and there was only just room enough left between to spread a hospital mattress of hay in the middle of the tent on the floor for me. I put my valise and trousers and coat for a pillow, and wrapped myself in a railway wrapper, and went to sleep.

Got up at 5 a.m. and went for a stroll in the neighbouring woods to hear the birds sing before breakfast. I heard a good deal of canonading going on towards Petersburg.

After breakfast I rode with Dr Doghearty to the rear of the camp to look for a place to establish a Corps Base Hospital, ready for the expected fight.

What a terrible scourge war is! The country is desolate. We saw some very fine houses, some burnt, others deserted, others occupied by women or troops. Women are allowed to remain unmolested, and are fed provided they take the oath of allegiance to U.S. All able men have fled. I saw a few old and sickly men left. It is very sad to see happy homes thus broken up. I went into some of the houses, and found them well furnished, evidently the property of people in easy circumstances. There was every appearance of easy comfort. But that was gone now; the carpets and furniture had been ill-used by the troops, flower gardens trodden down carelessly. It made me feel unhappy to see these nicely and carefully arranged flower beds so cruelly treated. I could not help imagining with what care and pleasure they had been cultivated by some ladies probably, who took a healthy pride in them. I thought of my Mother, and her garden, and I could not walk across them on the newly-made path out of respect to feelings which to my mind are sacred.

The tent where I slept last night, as well as the tents of most of the officers of the 2nd Army Corps, are pitched on the green field in front of one of the largest and finest houses in the country – the property of a Mr Jones, said to be a wealthy man and owner of a large estate. He has fled, but the ladies remain. Within fifteen paces in rear of my tent there is a plot of ground about four yards square, surrounded by iron rails ornamented. It is the family vault of the Joneses. The rails are now broken, and rubbish and filth have been thrown inside, without any respect for either the dead within, or the living relatives who are without, and in the house so near in sight. It seems so savage and barbarously cruel to trifle with sacred feelings unnecessarily.

As the field hospitals in this sector were empty, all the serious cases being immediately sent to City Point, Evans saw no useful purpose in staying.

July 6 1864.
Sleeping on the ground in a malaria district does not suit the present state of my health . . . I have seen all that is interesting . . . We are within a few hundred yards of the enemy lines, within easy range of a battery which is expected to open up on us at any moment now. I run the risk of being shot as much as anybody else. As I have no interest in the quarrel worth my while to run that risk, I have determined not to do so.
I wrote to General Meade after breakfast, requesting him to

send me somehow to City Point. There was not a troop horse to spare in the camp, because of the momentary expectation of an attack. General Humphries (sic) was good enough to lend me his own private horse and mounted orderly. While they were being got ready, I had a pleasant conversation with the General. He thinks that there are at present 120,000 men *actively* engaged in the two armies of Generals Meade and Butler. That is, all men on duty.

I returned to City Point in time to lunch with Dr Dalton. We came along a more shady road than the one we went by. All the country however was like what I saw before, laid waste by war, and materials of war scattered about. Dead animals here and there among the recent graves of soldiers, shot and shell told how the deed was done, the trees splintered, old clothes, belts, cartridge cases et cetera, everywhere, and the houses burnt or deserted. Desolation reigned . . . Dr Dalton gave me an introduction to Dr Mitchell, PMO of the Cavalry Corps Hospital. The hospital is very nicely situated on the Appotomax, and consists of a large number of tents of all kinds, long, square and bell-shaped. Dr Mitchell received me most hospitably, he ordered a marquee to be pitched for me, and furnished it with table, chair . . .

Evans was favourably impressed by the medical skill provided at rear hospitals which contrasted with the squalor of the field stations. However, he noted that casualties treated under canvas, with the advantage of fresh air, often made quicker recovery than those taken into stuffy wards, and succumbed less easily to disease.*

Between July 6 and July 20 Evans moved about among the Federal armies. One of the documents surviving from this fortnight is a stained and tattered pass:

Pass No 974. Headquarters of the Armies of the U.S. (The word "Potomac" had been crossed out and "U.S." written in).
Office Provost Marshall General. Armies operating against

*Disease was a greater menace than bullets or bayonets. Water and food were liable to contamination. It is significant that of the 359,528 Unionist soldiers who died in the war, about 200,000 succumbed not to wounds but to disease.

Richmond City. Pt. Va. July 9, 1864.
The bearer Dr Evans, Royal Artillery, has permission to pass
from these . . . to Washington D.C. This pass will expire July
12, 1864. By command Brigadier General Patrick, Provost
Marshall General.

It was signed by a Captain and an ADC, and, on the back, in the
same writing as the signature, is written: "Permit to take a rifle
and shield picked up on the field."

Evans evidently used this pass to make a quick dash back into
Washington to deposit his souvenirs and to refresh himself. He
spent the night of July 11 in Washington. During that night a
surprise attack was made on the capital by Southern troops.

I was wakened at night by a furious canonading and was told
that the enemy had come to the fort and that fighting was
going on. I obtained a horse, and went to see what there was
to see. By this time the enemy was said to be retreating, but
there were no troops in Washington to pursue them. I
followed them accompanied by an officer for some miles
until we reached the country house of the Postmaster General, which had been burned and the furniture thrown into
the garden. The Southern army had left a number of
wounded behind. I spoke with some of the medical officers
who had stayed behind to look after them.

On returning to the Federal lines, Evans spent almost a week as
the guest of the Commander-in-Chief, General Grant, to whom he
brought two letters of introduction, the one Dr Flint had given
him, the other, a powerful reinforcement, obtained from General
Butler. Unfortunately, the record of this visit which Evans made
in his diary has been lost* but in an interview with a journalist
many years later and in correspondence with John Drinkwater,
the dramatist, he made it clear that the General had been a
friendly host. They dined together at the same table and had
several conversations, long and short. During one of these talks,
Evans said he understood that the Northern forces were disor-

*The missing pages were among those believed to have been torn from the diary
by a journalist. These pages also covered Evans' subsequent visit to General
Thomas, and the description of this encounter was written in his later years.

ganised ("but I did not quote Lord Lyons as the authority for this statement."). General Grant replied, "Yes, of course we are disorganised, but we shall win."

I was with General Grant when he sent a cavalry brigade to cut the railway communications carrying supplies to the Southern armies.
The General told me that prisoners from the South had given information that every available man had been enlisted to fight with the Confederate army, "whereas we," said Grant, "are sure of getting recruits and can afford to lose ten to one so long as we can keep organised." I said that this seemed cruel. Grant agreed but said it was necessary in order to win.

Asked for his impressions of Grant, Evans said they were "all good". In old age he staunchly defended the General against the popular belief that he was a drunkard, declaring that during the several days he spent in his company he saw no sign and heard no evidence that Grant was anything but temperate.

While with Grant, Evans was again attacked by dysentery and the doctors advised him to return to Washington before the illness became worse. Accordingly, he set off, hoping to visit the headquarters of General Thomas on the way.

As he rode along, he joined three Union officers on a hilltop who were surveying the fighting through field glasses, "a splendid target for snipers".

One of them handed me the glasses so that I could see Robert E Lee's headquarters. As the American was describing the Southern General's positions, a bullet whizzed between us.
I returned the glasses, we separated, and rode away . . . But I was glad to have seen the headquarters of the great Confederate General who was such a hero to both sides.

On reaching the sector commanded by General Thomas, Evans found him in a trench, about to open an attack. When he

Katie aged 45 — "her gossipy tea parties became a legend".

Griff's daughter Erie, aged three. Later she devoted her life to him.

Griff's sister Eliza: "She must promise not to give the children wine".

Katie, a soldier's wife in Ipswich, with her two elder daughters.

Katie's photograph of Griff (right) and friends outside the Evans' quarters at Curragh Camp, Ireland

approached, proffering his pass and Dr Flint's letter of introduction, the General gave him a baleful look, seeming to be considerably put out at being confronted by a British officer. He glanced at the testimonials and handed them back.

"Nobody wearing a British uniform should expect a welcome here," he said. "British sympathies are all with Lee. But I suppose I can't throw out a friend of a friend."

I thanked him and said that although the sympathy of any British officer might be with Lee because he was entitled to fight for his native state of Virginia, yet Britain was, after all, officially neutral.

"Neutral!" said Thomas. "Take a look at that!" and he thrust a shell into my hands. "That is what landed on my breakfast table this morning. Well, what is it? Tell me."

I replied that it looked like a dud shell. "Dud shell!" said the General. "Yes, it's a dud shell. If it was not a dud I wouldn't be here now. Tell me who made it?"

I turned it over and saw that it was made by Whitworth and Co. "Can you deny that is a British shell and made by a British firm?" Thomas demanded.

"I cannot deny the evidence of my own eyes, sir!" I said. "I suppose my country cannot prevent private firms from supplying the South with ammunition. I promise to report what I have seen to the British Ambassador in Washington."

Evans then asked if he might be permitted to observe the battle for a while, adding, "You and I are both Welshmen, sir." This did not please the General, who said that he had lost all connection with Wales, had no Welsh sympathies and did not know a word of the Welsh language. Then he added, "I have no more time for you. You can either stay in the trench with me or go aloft with the men signalling the range. Take your pick!"

Evans decided to join the signalmen. He mounted a raised platform and stood with an officer who was directing a barrage by the Northern battery. After a while he withdrew and continued his journey.

My thoughts were with the Southern commander. Not one

officer or soldier had spoken a word against this gallant enemy. They described Robert E Lee as "the best general in the world except for our own General Grant," and as "a perfect gentleman and Christian."

As he rode towards the river where he hoped to get a steamer bound for Hampton Roads, he began to plan the report he had promised to give to President Lincoln. He had been allowed to examine patients and look at hospitals wherever he went and had written copious notes. Aboard the river steamer he was glad to lie down, dozing fitfully in a post-febrile condition, and thought he was "in heaven, listening to an angel choir". Then he realised that there were actually people singing on the steamer. He was hearing one of the first river boat negro spiritual concerts in its natural setting.

I had never heard such musical voices before. I felt my way between the decks till I came upon a crowd of negroes singing hymns. They told me they had been released by the Northerners and were on their way to employment. They had been warned by their Southern masters that if the Northerners got them they would shut them up somewhere with snakes. "Is that true?" they asked me. I assured them it was not.

At Hampton Roads he called on his friends in the frigate "Phaeton," "the Captain and Commander and all the officers giving me a hearty welcome and furnishing a comfortable bunk for me". Continuing his journey, he made a detour to Arlington, the beautiful estate overlooking Washington, which had been confiscated from General Lee and turned into a "free man's village" for negroes. He visited the hospital there and met an old negro who claimed that he could recite the whole of the Old Testament, beginning anywhere.

He told me that his former Massa's little boy had taught him to read as they played together. He said he had later found an Old Testament on a rubbish heap and committed it to memory. He longed to have a New Testament, and on my return to Canada I posted him one.

The "free man's village" was a collection of temporary wooden huts some distance from Lee's house which was guarded. Evans was refused admission. He then returned to Washington.

Washington, *July 20, 1864*
Professor Henry had invited me to his house at 5 p.m. to take me to visit the President at his country residence, hoping to find him disengaged and to spend the evening with him.

On our way we saw President Lincoln in his carriage at a distance of about 200 yards, returning home escorted by twenty mounted men. I am told he is persuaded to take this escort because his life would be in danger otherwise from Southern sympathisers.

Before calling on him, we visited the Soldiers' Home in the grounds. We found there eighty men, wounded and pensioned, belonging to the regular army, taking their supper. The grounds were very beautiful commanding a splendid view of Washington and the valley of the Potomac.

Unfortunately, while we were thus loitering, the Secretary for War came to see the President on some urgent business, and Mr Lincoln sent us word that he was extremely sorry in not being able to see us, and requested us to call again tomorrow or any other evening.

Evans had to start for Montreal next day, at latest by evening, as his leave was expiring. He was most anxious to make his report to the President, so Professor Henry said he would try to arrange an early morning interview in the more official atmosphere of the White House.

Accordingly, at eight next morning, he met Evans, and, on their way to the White House, took him to see the Treasury and the Lighthouse Board offices.

Washington, *July 21, 1864*

About 9.30 a.m. we called on the President at the White House because I have no time to go again to his country house. He received us very kindly, but as there were many people waiting before we arrived to see him on official business, we only remained a few minutes.

In appearance he is what is termed a tall, lanky Yankee, his upper eyelids drop partly over his eyes, his lower lip is very prominent. He has a "knowing" smile which, however, is not unpleasant. He shows marks of mental overwork which reminded me of what Lord Lyons told me the other evening: "Mr Lincoln is not the man to look at that he was four years ago".

It is very remarkable the absence of all formality or insignia of office in this country. There was nothing about the President or his official residence to show that he was different from an ordinary subject – a banker or a broker. There was no military guard at the office, nor did I see any man about in Livery. The White House is not at all a grand place; very little of it appeared to be furnished. The "Grand Reception Room" and some others I saw were very seedy looking . . ."

The rest of the diary entry has been lost, but in later years Evans said that he had told the President he had seen no sign of alcoholism or indiscipline amongst the troops; that he was impressed with their firm determination to conquer, but he had observed no vindictive feelings; he quoted the praises he had continually heard of General Robert E Lee.

One can imagine the smile that would hover on Lincoln's expressive face at the ingenuousness of this young officer who imagined that on the strength of a few weeks at the front he could tell the President anything about his army's morale that he did not already know!

President Lincoln appeared to be pleased, but because of the number of people waiting to see him, he brought the interview to an end before I had even started to tell him the content of my medical notes.

Later that evening, Evans left Washington on his journey back to Montreal.

The memory of President Lincoln, who was assassinated nine months later, remained vivid in Griffith Evans' mind for the rest of his life.

During his few days in Washington, he had visited a military hospital which the President had inspected the previous day. One of the doctors there told him a story Evans was often to repeat as an example of Lincoln's quick wit, tact and humanity.

The doctor said that he had taken the President into a ward where amongst the patients was a soldier whose scrotum had been shot away. A wealthy lady patron, who often visited the hospital, and was in the habit of asking awkward questions, had been standing near this soldier's bed demanding that the doctors and nurses should inform her what was the matter with him, as he himself would not. She walked up to the President and complained that nobody would tell her, least of all the patient himself. "Perhaps he will tell *me*," said Lincoln, and strolled over to the man's bedside. After a brief conversation he returned and said, "Well, ma'am, all I can tell you is, that if you had been standing where he was at the precise moment when he was hit, you would not have been hurt at all."

CHAPTER TEN

Religion under the Microscope

Evans was soon to pay the penalty for ignoring the doctor's warning that by undertaking his American adventure he would be severely jeopardising his health. When he returned to Montreal, congestion had developed in his lungs as a result of his reduced vitality after repeated attacks of dysentery and the strain to which he had put his body in the July heat of Virginia. The medical officer diagnosed pneumonia and ordered him into the military hospital. But first he was able to give the MO a brief account of his experiences. The doctor later confessed that when Evans told him that he had met President Lincoln and the various Northern Generals, he attributed the story to the imaginings of a delirious mind, but when he looked at the diaries, official passes and other souvenirs, which his patient had entrusted to his care, he realised that it must be true, and, as requested, repeated the facts to the commanding officer.

Pneumonia was only the start of Griff's sufferings. He had further violent symptoms and the doctors told him he had developed "sporadic cholera". (It was later reported to him that after a few days the doctors diagnosed typhoid fever as well).

On his 29th birthday, the brigade doctors were struggling to save his life. His skin had turned grey, he endured agonising cramps, was suffering intense thirst and was gasping for breath. It was feared he could not last the day. He rallied and there was brief hope of his recovery. That night, however, the senior physician was summoned back to his bedside. Evans had moments of consciousness, and during one of these the doctors felt it their duty to warn him that he was now likely to die and to bid him state any wishes which they would see discharged. But he passed into delirium.

During a brief return to consciousness I heard voices. One

92

said, "It was madness to attempt such a journey," and another said, "If he lives it will be months before he can return." At that moment I resolved to live.

His will to survive and his strong constitution pulled him through – to live for another 71 years.
For a while, his illness affected his memory.

To recover it I disciplined myself as I lay in bed to short periods of memory training. I grouped ideas and facts into batches and repeated them to myself. I did a little more each day until, after some weeks, I could recite verses and recall prescriptions for various ailments affecting horses.

He reached the state of convalescence when the MO ordered him a daily mug of porter. Griff objected and insisted, if he must take it, that the doses and times be prescribed as for any medicine and the effect of the alcohol content on the blood noted. The porter treatment was abandoned.

When the battery was transferred to Toronto, Evans went too, but he was not taken off the sick list until several weeks later. His illness had left him low in spirits and lethargic. He spent much time reading or copying morbid verses into his journal, and went for long solitary walks by Lake Ontario.

As his strength returned, he felt the need for a leisure activity to replace his recent medical studies at McGill. He found an outlet for his mental energy first in the study of religion and later, also, in medical research.

He called himself a freethinker – "not so much an agnostic as a rationalist" – and always had a deep interest in other people's beliefs. As a Victorian and a Welshman, he had a profound respect for the value of religion as an influence on human behaviour, and though he did not feel that he needed any specific form of organised religion, he believed that other people did. Indeed, he occasionally helped with Bible class and Sunday school work, as this letter to his father shows:

June 19 1863
There are several Welsh vessels in port now. I had about an

hour's chat last evening with two captains in the cabin of a
vessel from Aberystwyth: the Brig "Hannah" (Captain
Humphreys). He says he knows Dr Pughe well. He seems
fond of talking and discussing religious subjects. I hope we
shall have a profitable Ysgol Sul next Sunday out of three or
four Welsh crews, each being ten or twelve in number . . . As
I have to attend a Bible class of our men this afternoon, I
must now conclude.
Your affectionate
Griff

In another letter at that time to his father, Griff wrote scath-
ingly about the attitude of certain ministers of the Congregational
Church to the Civil War – the church in which he had been
brought up.

During the past week or nine days, the Congregational
Union was held in this city, Montreal. There were ministers
delegated from several of the Northern states. It was most
remarkable that every one of them was so full of the "war
spirit" that they had nothing else to speak about. Instead of
informing the assembly about the state of the churches in
the states which they represented, they all spoke of the war
to justify the Northern cause. They said that peace with the
Southerners is now out of the question. It must be fought
out *until the whole population of the South is exterminated*, and
the Northern soldiers are to be remunerated by the Southern states being divided among them!
Moreover, these evangelical (question mark) ministers said
that they rejoiced to think that the united (Northern) states
made no objection to the enlistment of clergymen and
ministers as active soldiers, so that if necessary they could
take up arms and lead their congregations to war or victory,
or die in such a glorious effort! So much for Yankee Christ-
endom!

The nineteenth century saw the rise of several breakaway sects,
and Griff had plenty of opportunity to examine the latest new
beliefs in a young, developing country. Brought up on the motto
"To everyone an opinion", he did his probing with tolerance. He

94

even tried to overcome his innate dislike of Roman Catholicism; indeed, years later he was moved to say, "You could call me a Jesuit if the name had not been brought into disrepute." In Toronto he formed a friendship with the Roman Catholic chaplain; they met alternately at Griff's quarters in the barracks and in the priest's room at the convent.

> We discussed the New Testament, the authority claimed by the R.C. Church and the value of tradition. The priest reported these talks to his Bishop who gave him books for me to read.

As a result of these talks, however, it was not Griff but the priest who showed signs of change of heart, and eventually the Bishop decided that he must be removed from Griff's orbit. Griff was touched by his friend's distress on parting but it does not seem to have occurred to him that he himself may have contributed to the man's agony of mind.

> When I went to the convent to bid him farewell . . . he told me there was a secret weighing on his mind, and he must relieve himself by telling me though he would have to do penance of the Church for doing so. It was this: he often felt during and after our weekly discussion that if he allowed himself to reason on religious subjects as I did, he would not remain in the Church another day. He would rather earn his living by menial labour. But he could not now cease trusting his faith. He was brought up for the Church since babyhood . . . It was not possible for one like me to imagine the power of all that prevented him from reasoning continuously upon religious subjects. In parting he took my hand in both his, sobbed, and wiped tears flowing over it. I felt deeply affected. He was a good man. I am sure our fatherly God accepted him as a son.

The implication of the last sentence seems to be that God would forgive the priest his Roman Catholicism!

In Montreal, earlier, Griff made friends with some Irvingites, a sect he had first come across in Bridgnorth.

What fascinated me about these people was that they really believed Jesus would return in person any day. They had to be constantly expectant. Some of my friends had a spare table, chair et cetera at every meal.

Griff was also interested in the Plymouth Brethren whom he admired for their simple, world-renouncing piety and their rejection of any professional, ordained ministry. He blamed John Nelson Darby, a barrister who gave his life to evangelical work, for the breaking off of the exclusive sect from the main open sect.

Some of my best friends in Canada were Plymouth Brethren of the liberal (open) kind, till Mr Darby came to demand them to be more strictly narrow and exclusive. He received the hospitality of my friends and I conversed with him often. When I disagreed with him, he told me bluntly that it was because the Holy Ghost did not teach me.

Among the many Christians Griff met in Canada none perhaps was quite so devout as Lord Adelbert Cecil, son of the second Marquess of Exeter and a lieutenant in the Rifle Brigade. In 1864, before returning to England on extended leave, Lord Adelbert asked Griff's advice on a matter that was causing him some anxiety. Should he dare to tell his godmother, Queen Victoria, that he "thought she had failed him by not warning him of the temptations he would have to meet in the army?"

Griff replied that he saw no reason for not speaking to his godmother on so solemn a subject simply because she was a Queen. Adelbert later wrote from England: "My dear Evans, I hope you will correspond with me occasionally and tell me about the goings-on of my regiment as I have no-one in it to tell me anything . . ." When Griff recovered from his illness Adelbert, now back in Canada, told him of his interview with the Queen, which, he said, took place at Windsor in December 1864.

Adelbert knelt before her Majesty and asked permission to speak. She put her hand on his shoulder and said "Speak out, my boy, and confide all you have to say to me." Adelbert said he then told the Queen that he did not think she had done her duty as his godmother because she had not told him of the gospel.

"What do you mean by the gospel?" asked the Queen.

"The truth about Christ coming to save sinners and that we are all requiring converting, and how small a thing it is to belong to any church, and how little a thing the differences between the churches are as compared with this great truth," said Adelbert.

To judge by the account of this interview which Lord Adelbert gave to Griff, the Queen seems to have sensed that in some way her godson was overwrought, for she told him very kindly to get up, and said, "Well, dear boy, if I have failed in my duty I hope you will forgive me." Griff's account concludes: "I told Adelbert he had done right to confide in the Queen".*

Two of the many subjects which attracted Evans' wide-ranging curiosity during his years in Canada were astronomy and hypnotism. Many years later, he used to tell his grandchildren that under the instruction of a Montreal friend named Baker, an amateur astronomer, he had been awed by the realisation that he had witnessed the ending of a star which had actually burned itself out many light years before.

> Mr Baker lent me books on astronomy and allowed me to use his four-inch telescope. One night, in 1866, he hastened to my quarters and asked me to return with him to see if I noticed anything unusual in a certain constellation. I agreed that I could see a star which I had not noticed before. "That's it!" said Baker. "I wanted confirmation." He wrote to the local paper reporting a new star and later wrote to the Astronomer Royal, enclosing an affidavit which he asked me to sign, claiming to be the first to see the star, which eventually disappeared.**

Evans delved into hypnotism under the tuition of a certain George Washington Stone who later solemnly presented him with a "diploma". Dated 1869, the "diploma" affirmed that Dr

*In 1868 Lord Adelbert resigned his commission and became a lay evangelist with the Plymouth Brethren, writing a number of books. He was later drowned in the St Lawrence when a vessel capsized.

**Invited to give his views, a student of astronomy says that what Baker and Evans saw was probably a supernova which appeared in Corona Borealis and could have been observed from that part of Canada. There is, he adds, no record that Mr Baker was first in the world to see it.

Griffith Evans was now qualified to practise "electro-biology" and mesmerism; it also entitled him to "apply the power derived from a knowledge of animal magnetism to the relief of pain or the cure of disease."

Evans seems earlier to have sensed the possibilities of electro-therapy though he never had the opportunity to pursue the subject. Years later, he sent his so-called diploma to his doctor daughter, Erie, with this comment:

You may be amusingly surprised by my "diploma" which you may destroy as of no use. G.W. Stone was of good reputation. He was chief assistant of Lord Bulwer Lytton in the investigation of spiritualism. Stone told us privately that he personally did not believe in spiritualism.

In old age, Griff used to say that Christ was the greatest hypnotist of all time. He also recalled how Stone had been threatened with a horsewhip in a public thoroughfare by a man whom Stone had hypnotised before a large audience. "As the man approached with the whip, Stone commanded him to dance on one foot, which the victim did to the amusement of a growing crowd."

Griff's interest in the possibilities of "electro-biology" originated in an incident which occurred during his earlier years in Montreal.

I had injured my wrist when thrown from my big grey mare. Next day, in great pain, I attended a lecture on Old Testament prophets at Nordheimer's Hall. I sat near the door so that I could get out if the pain became unbearable. I could hardly hold a feather between the thumb and finger. Suddenly, I thought I saw the Principal Veterinary Surgeon, Mr Wilkinson – whom I knew to be in England – walk in at the door. I was so astonished that I felt thoroughly electrified, as I had felt standing on an insulated stool handling an electric machine, feeling my hair erect . . . I perspired immediately and felt something flow steadily from my spine down my right arm to the tips of my fingers, and return in the same manner. The pain stopped instantly and was never renewed. Before the lecture ended I could press and pinch hard with my right thumb and finger.

In 1867, Dr James Bovell, a teacher at the University, and one of Toronto's leading medical men, invited Dr Evans to join him in medical research at Trinity College. Griff's military duties seem to have been undemanding at this period, and he was able to spend much of his time on research. In 1868, Bovell engaged a nineteen-year-old assistant named William Osler, a son of the manse, born on the edge of the upper Canadian wilderness, who was studying medicine at Trinity. Griff described him as "a young man of great charm" with a keen intellect and great analytical ability. He took him under his wing and gave him all possible encouragement, his favourite greeting being, "And how is the young man to-day?" In this way began a relationship which developed into a warm friendship with one of the most brilliant, versatile and distinguished men in the history of British medicine.

Osler has been known to generations of practitioners as the author of "Principles and Practice of Medicine", considered by some to be the most popular text book in the English language. As Sir William Osler F R S., regius professor of Medicine at Oxford, he said that he had been inspired as a youth by Dr Griffith Evans who had taught him to use the microscope, explaining "Treat it gently, as you would a lady." Osler's wide range of achievements included pioneer work on tuberculosis which was one of his special interests. He was among the first to give tuberculin a thorough clinical trial. He also seriously questioned the established use of alcohol in medical practice, and pointed out that its regular prescription increased the danger of tuberculosis. Undoubtedly, this was one direction in which he had been inspired by Evans who had recently shown the way to enlightened thinking on the treatment of tuberculosis and also never ceased to voice his deep mistrust of the use of alcohol. The echoes of Evans' sayings ring down through Osler's teaching.

Shortly before Osler's death, he greeted his old friend, Evans, then a hale and hearty octogenarian: "And how is the young man to-day?"

CHAPTER ELEVEN

Marriage

In the spring of 1869, after eight years in Canada, Griff returned to Wales on leave. After staying for a few days with his parents at Tŷ Mawr, he set off on a long solitary walk among the Welsh mountains. From Caernarvon he walked by way of Nant Ffrancon and Capel Curig to Bala. Then he struck over the hills to Montgomeryshire – and to Katie Jones.

He knew that both Katie's parents had recently died, but it was only when he returned to Wales that he discovered that she was not only still unwed but had no-one in mind. Griff was almost 34, an age when bachelors are becoming less likely to marry in haste. Katie's long silence, following the coolness of her last letters, must have made him hesitate to approach her again, and the purpose of his lone walk was to resolve his own mind and his bachelor misgivings about marriage.

He arrived at Llanfaircaereinion at dusk and went at once to what had been the doctor's house, which had an empty, deserted look, (the brass plate had been removed from the door). He knocked and presently a glimmer of light appeared in the front room where patients used to wait to see the doctor when he was sober enough to treat them. Suddenly the door opened and Katie stood, holding a lamp aloft, as she had done when he first visited her home nine years before. What happened when she recognised him in the light of her lamp is a story later told to her daughters by Katie herself.

Soon after her mother's death, her father had drunk himself into his grave, and Katie had gone to live with relatives in Towyn. She had now returned briefly to what was for her a house of sadness to arrange for its disposal.

She gave Griff a simple supper, as she had done on her first visit, and then they talked about their lives during their long separation. For Katie, who was now 25, the years had been devoted to nursing her parents. Each of them confessed to misunderstandings; each had imagined that the other had lost interest and found romance elsewhere, he because of her long silence, she because of the photograph she had seen at Tŷ Mawr, showing him with another girl.

That night Griff stayed at the village inn. Next morning (it was April 1) he proposed to her as they walked beside the River Banwy.

When, years later, Griff was serving in India, Katie wrote:

> While you were in Canada, I made myself unhappy raising some ghosts; it was because I did not know you.

She also confessed that "when you proposed I wished you had been a bit more off your head, and not so cool and collected!"

Griff had to serve a further year in Canada, and they decided that they would not marry until he returned. Meanwhile, Katie would continue to live with her uncle and aunt, William and Mary Rees, in Towyn.

Before he left, he sat with her in Aunt Rees' parlour, a large Bible open between them. They were seeking a text appropriate for her alcoholic father's tombstone. They chose a verse from Psalm 119: "It is good for me that I have been in trouble that I may learn thy statutes."

When Griff returned to Canada, he took with him a lock of Katie's brown hair.

His regiment, now back in Montreal, had to deal with another Fenian rising. He was awarded the Canadian General Service Medal with two bars. Then, at last, on July 6, 1870, the battery embarked for England in the troopship "Crocodile" – "sent specially because HRH Prince Arthur is returning with the Rifle Brigade". The Prince, Griff observed, "is almost teetotal."

July 16 1870
The Royal yacht, "Victoria and Albert", met us in the English Channel, sent by the Queen, who is staying at Osborne, especially to take Prince Arthur to her . . . .. Prince Arthur left us off Hurst Castle. The Captain of the yacht informèd us that FRANCE HAD DECLARED WAR AGAINST PRUSSIA.

101

Because of the menacing situation in Europe, Griff was detained at Woolwich for two more frustrating months; then, in September, the battery moved to Ipswich, and he told Katie she could prepare for the wedding. When he was re-united with her on October 21, he said that for him no religious rite was necessary. "I should be happy with a gypsy wedding or a Red Indian one." But Katie did want a religious rite and all the traditional customs. He agreed to their being married by the Calvinist Minister at Bethel Chapel, Towyn, but insisted that they get away from the celebrations without delay.

October 26 1870
Married at 8 a.m. left by the 9.10 a.m. train. We were alone at last in a first-class compartment. Arrived at Caernarvon for dinner, then visited the Castle.

In Towyn the legend grew that Griffith Evans had actually abducted his bride, and, indeed, there must have been shaking of heads when he whisked her away without so much as a glance at the wedding breakfast prepared for them.

Forty years earlier Evan Evans had also taken his bride to Caernarvon.

On that occasion my parents went to see Telford's suspension bridge. Now Katie and I were able to see Stephenson's new Britannia Bridge which conveys the railway to Holyhead.

Katie might have preferred her groom's mind to be dwelling on less prosaic matters than the Menai bridges. Their visit proved more dramatic than they would have wished. They wandered past the stone lions guarding the entrance to the dark interior of the tubular bridge.

We were strolling between the rails when we heard a terrible roar and not one but two trains bore down upon us, one from the Island of Anglesey and one from the mainland, so that we were trapped between the two. I clasped Katie to me and shouted into her ear. "Stay perfectly still!" We clung together, her head buried in my coat, in the narrow space between the up and down lines. The two shrieking monsters rushed past us on either side like flaming dragons, and the wind of their passing lifted my hair and blew out the ribbons of Katie's bonnet.

The wedding had inspired the Welsh bard, Black Robin of Snowdon – more commonly known as Mr Robert Parry of Prospect Villa, Abergavenny – to write an *englyn* for the couple. "Two fine families were united," sang Robin in his Welsh verse, little knowing how the two families had nearly been disunited!

Before the newly-weds left for Ipswich, they were photographed, the bride a pretty, cuddlesome girl, wearing a wifely bonnet; the groom somewhat thin and thoughtful (in a photograph taken a year later, he looks much better fed).

Modern psychiatrists, astrologers or marriage counsellors might say that there was every reason for the union of Griffith Evans and Katie Jones to end in disaster. They married the one knowing very little of the other, for, apart from some childhood meetings, they had spent only a few days in each other's company, and their correspondence had been desultory. In tastes and personality they had little in common. Griff was serious-minded, intolerant of small talk, meticulous and purposeful, having the utmost integrity. Katie had charm; she was quick-witted, talkative, mischievous, with a sparkling humour. She loved people, was impatient about details ("I can't be bothered with fiddle-de-dee"), a sin in Griff's estimation. She was, indeed, beguilingly feminine; nor had she been tarnished by those nine dreary years of caring for her parents. Yet these two dissimilar people remained devoted to each other for the rest of their lives.

They had seven years together before they were parted again, living first in Ipswich, then in London, then in Ireland. Their first home was Richmond Cottage, Waterloo Road, Ipswich, and here, after eleven months, their first child was born. She was named Myfanwy Wynona, and in her honour, Griff's father – as he did for each of his many grandchildren – composed an *englyn*.

Before Griff went abroad again, Katie bore him two more daughters, Erie and Towena (when his daughters were old enough to lament their names, Griff said that names *ought* to be unusual or they lost their point).

The erstwhile bachelor became an exceedingly proud father, earnestly concerned with every detail of his firstborn child's welfare. Katie later said that, in their early years of married life, Griff's droll seriousness sometimes made her laugh "till the tears ran down her face".

This caused him to be alarmed less there was something amiss with my tear ducts and he said he must examine them – and this made me laugh all the more.

Griff bought a large notebook which he called Wynona's Diary; he wrote the diary in the first person, as if it were the baby speaking, and no fact was too trivial to record – how many inches she had grown, how her vaccination took, what gifts she received. He expected Katie to continue the diary when they were separated. In the spring of 1872, her husband was transferred to the Army Service Corps and posted to Woolwich, and Katie went back to Wales while Griff was finding a house for them. She really could not be bothered with Wynona's diary, but to please him she made one or two entries:

May 27 1872
Aunt Jane has made me a pretty yellow pelisse. Janet Powell came to see me and brought a pretty white frock.
June 1.
Left Llanfaircaereinion and arrived Woolwich. Father met us at Euston and welcomed us very heartily. Lizzy the maid-servant came with us. Father had bought me a crib and a very nice, comfortable perambulator.

Then Griff resumed the diary until:

August 2 1872
Dada left for the autumnal manoeuvres. Marched with the companies *en route* for Blandford to join the southern armies.

Wynona, the supposed author of that entry, was then eleven months old. But at least the diary gives interesting glimpses of Griff and Katie's life in Victorian London:

September 22 1872
Dada returned this afternoon very unexpected. He was to come next Wednesday. Mother was delighted to see him and so was I, after second thoughts. I did not remember who he was until he took me in his arms. He then gave me such a pretty toy – he said I had grown into a beautiful child, that he was very fond of me, and of Mother.

October 8
Dada and Mam took the servants to see the Crystal Palace, Sydenham, to-day, driving the wagonette. As the house was locked up, no-one to take charge of it. I had to be taken to see the Palace too . . . I couldn't help laughing at the monkeys. I was not a bit afraid of them . . . The parrots screeched . . . The servants were bewildered at seeing so many strange things.

Mother told father she heard some ladies say I was a wonderfully pretty child, and I fancy she thinks I was the most interesting, if not the most beautiful, object to look at in the Palace. Father says it was because I was a good child, did not cry or be frightened, for all children become very ugly when they are naughty.

November 26
I was very sick last week (teeth) but Dada says I suffered only moderately. Mama says my eyes grow to be like those of her mother.

After November, the diary was neglected; Griff too busy; Katie too concerned with practical matters, including pregnancy.

July 12 1873
Many things have happened to me since November. I have had six new teeth. I have learned to walk and run. I can say "Wynona", "more", "up-a-da", "down", "puss". I should like to have had it recorded when I first walked and learned to say the words. Mama undertook to write it for me, but she

always put it off.

Now I have got Dada to write what an interesting event has happened to me, for this morning my little sister was born, so that I am no more the baby. Dada says she is *my* baby. I was taken in to see her in bed with dear Mama this afternoon. I was so surprised to see anyone smaller than myself that I did not know what to do. But she was so pretty, with her little hands and nose and mouth which I pointed out to Dada, and then she opened her eyes as if she looked at me, and I laughed with delight, and I kissed dear Mama for her, and I kissed her too. I tried to stroke her face, but Dada, fearing I would hurt her prevented me. My sister's name is Erie.

Katie, with two small children to care for, continued to neglect Wynona's diary, and was once more rebuked:

February 14 1874
Many months have passed since Mama recorded anything in my diary and I have forgotten many things that happened. I can talk pretty well, and for more than two months I have been taking my meals with Dada and Mama. Dada bought me a chair and I behave very well generally. But sometimes I upset my milk and talk more than I ought, and then I am sent away from table . . .

Throughout his years of home service, Griff continued to expand his medical knowledge, engaging in research work at Ipswich Infirmary, and, in London, studying histology and experimental physiology at King's College, as well as ophthalmology at Moorfields; but despite what must, by the standards of his day, have been a considerable medical knowledge he seemed to have no wish to make use of it in general practice. He treated but few patients, apart from family and friends. In Ipswich, however, he treated a case of tetanus under dramatic circumstances similar to those when Louis Pasteur took responsibility for a child bitten by a mad dog.

One day the young son of a sergeant in my battery was

knocked down in the street by a dog cart, the wheel of which passed over his head, wounding him severely. He was carried to the Infirmary unconscious.

His mother came to me that evening in her distress, begging me to treat him if she brought him home. I persuaded her to leave him where he was, promising to see him every day.

I found that the boy had tetanus, and I was invited by the other doctors to a consultation. Asked for my opinion, I said I regarded the disease as a fever due to some specific cause for which there was no known remedy.*

Like other specific fevers it had to run its course. I said our duty was to keep the patient in the best possible position for self-recovery; that was, to favour as much easy rest as possible, to avoid everything that might excite the spasm, keep in a dark, silent room, no noise from without or within, give no food of any kind, nor any medicine, but let the patient drink water ad lib. No one should go in to see him except a specially selected nurse and the house-surgeon.

The other doctors protested strongly at the suggestion that no medicine should be administered, although they had no idea what to prescribe. Griff, who disliked the hypocrisy of giving placebos in such circumstances, doubtless expressed himself in no uncertain terms. Then, after further discussion:

I was asked would I venture the risk if I were made responsible for the treatment. I replied that I would, without hesitation, if I had the consent of the parent.

They all agreed for me to take charge of the case, the patient remaining in the Infirmary. The mother was called in, the subject was explained to her, the fatality of previous cases et cetera, and she expressed her willingness to comply with any treatment I recommended, and promised also for her husband.

The case recovered.

It is the only case of tetanus I ever had to treat in man, but I have treated a number of cases in horses on the same principle, and all recovered.

*This was some 14 years before the cause of tetanus was demonstrated.

The early years of Griff and Katie's married life were over-shadowed by the anxiety he felt for his family. Tŷ Mawr had become a place of sadness, no longer the cheerful, bustling farm-house of his childhood. His parents were infirm, half blind. His sister Maria was not the pretty girl he remembered. She had married one of her father's labourers, John Jones, who had taken over responsibility for the farm. Maria, the mother of three boys, was now the actual mistress of Tŷ Mawr, but the burden was proving too much for her frail body. Griff had also found his elder sister living in some hardship. Her husband, Griffith Dedwydd, had started a baby almost every time he returned from a long voyage. Eliza, her seven sons and one daughter were crowded into a tiny cottage at Barmouth. Griff decided to buy a house for them at Portmadoc* so that she and her family might have the use of it; it was large enough, also, to provide a refuge for his parents when they had to leave Tŷ Mawr.

Then, in the autumn of 1873, came the blow which the family had been dreading. Charles Edwards of Dolgelly, the owner of the rented land which Evan Evans had farmed for so long, announced that he intended to sell, offering possession the fol-lowing March 25 when the lease expired. The auctioneers' catalogue (Griff preserved a copy among his papers) read:

363 acres of excellent arable meadow, pasture and uplands. The farms are occupied by Evan Evans who has held the same upon leases which will expire by Lady Day next, when greatly increased rents may be obtained. A stream runs through the property . . . Views from every part of this fine estate over Cardigan Bay and Caernarvonshire . . .

Evan Evans, now 72, was adamant: he would not leave Tŷ Mawr; nothing would persuade him to leave. He would farm the pitiful remnant of 23 acres which were his own property.

In the event, the new owner invited the capable John Jones to

*The house, called Trem-y-Don, in Ralph Street, Borth-y-Gêst, Portmadoc, is still owned by Eliza's descendants. Griff had sold it to his only niece, Gwendydd and her husband, on Eliza's death in 1895. Among Griff's souvenirs was a letter from one of Eliza's sons, Evan Owen Dedwydd, "written in E.O's blood" and signed by all his brothers. Captain Evan Dedwydd became a sailor of considerable renown, and, at the turn of the century, established a new Atlantic record when he sailed his schooner "Theda" from Cape Cod to Gibraltar.

become his farm manager and this meant that, on the surface, life at Tŷ Mawr could continue more or less unchanged. But the landlord began to build a fine, modern house on the other side of the stream only a hundred yards from Tŷ Mawr. For old Evan this was a bitter humiliation. He was no longer the local squire; his former labourer had become the employee of the wealthy landowner whose big new house would reduce Tŷ Mawr to the status of a farm cottage.

The ailing Maria still had to bear the brunt of the farmhouse labour. But only for a year.

In the autumn of 1874 Griff had been posted to the Curragh Camp, near Dublin, and it was there the following April, that he received, a telegram announcing Maria's death. Her body had succumbed to the strain and anxiety of caring for husband, children and ailing parents.

Griff was stricken with grief. Katie recalled later how he wept in her arms and how at that moment she came to a fuller understanding of the depth of his feelings.

His parents were at last persuaded to leave Tŷ Mawr: they went to live with Eliza at Portmadoc. But they were deeply unhappy at being uprooted from the home they had known for so many years. Two years later, when Griff told old Mary Evans that he was being sent to India, she sank into a deep depression, and on July 11, 1877, died. Among Griff's personal possessions he included an envelope containing a lock of her hair; it was marked "Dear mother's hair, cut August 31, 1872."

Katie had long known that Griff was destined for further service abroad and sadly accepted the penalty of being married to a soldier under orders to serve in India. Life there was too hazardous for very young children so she must stay behind. She decided that she would take the three little girls to live with her uncle and aunt in Towyn.

In September 1877, Griff was gazetted back to the Royal Artillery and given a month's leave in which to prepare to embark. Just before they left the Curragh, they were visited by Meyrick, home on leave from India. It was the first time Katie had met her husband's bachelor friend; they took to each other from the start, and, in the next few years, Katie was forever suggesting to Griff the names of suitable brides for Meyrick.

Helped by his friend, Griff made a methodical list of the tropical kit he proposed to take to India, heading it "Memo Troopship."

This was his list:

3 white trousers, 1 cloak and cape, 1 cardigan jacket (to go in box with ulster) 6 merino shirts, 2 undress trousers, 3 flannel, 3 silk vests, 3 merino drawers, 1 helmet, 1 forage cap, 1 veil, 7 dinner napkins, 2 bath towels, 2 toilet towels, 6 silk pocket handkerchiefs, 1 *cane* – seat deckchair (carpet seats get dirty) 2 pairs of boots, 1 pair of slippers, 2 spectacles, white and black, 6 pairs of cotton socks, 1 box of safety matches and a few small wax tapers to light in cabin in emergency.

The most precious item of luggage was his new microscope, a fine model he had bought to take to India.

The parting came on October 30, 1877. Griff left to join her Majesty's troopship "Jumna", Katie waving on Towyn platform until the train was out of sight.

CHAPTER TWELVE

An Army Vet in India

Alexandria *November 1877*
Here I am, Katie *bach,* in the Mediterranean Sea, surrounded by all that is sacred in ancient history. Homer's Iliad and Odyssey, Virgil's Aeneas, the Phoenicians, the ships of Tarsus, the Holy Land . . . These countries are now the dark places of the earth. England is the focus of all that is civilising and good to regenerate the world.

Earlier that year the Queen had been proclaimed Empress of India. Britain bestrode the world. But (Griff wrote to Katie) "if the Empire is to survive it must produce men worthy of their responsibilities as guardians of civilisation."

The rest of his long letter to his wife is in lighter vein. It seems that Evans the iconoclast – in "Jumna" as in "The Great Eastern" several years before – railed at the dogma of the ship's padre.

We have a very high clergyman on board . . . I was so sickened by his nonsensical ways that I sat down through the whole service after the first hymn . . . I had tea directly after to soothe me, then I went on the upper deck for fresh air. There I found two officers sitting down smoking. They were talking about ritualism, and the following conversation will amuse you:
Officer No 1 I don't believe men worship God by mummery like that. Read the Sermon on the Mount. That's my religion. You know the Sermon on the Mount?
Officer No 2 No, I don't. What does it say?
Officer No 1 Good God, have you never read the Sermon on the Mount?
Officer No 2 I don't remember. Who is it by?

Officer No 1 (to me) You know where it is, don't you? I'll be hanged if I haven't forgotten the chapter, but it is somewhere in John.
I (to Officer No 1) No, it is in Matthew. It commences in the fifth chapter.
Officer No 1 At any rate, you ought to read it. The substance of it is: Love God, honour the Queen and do to others as you would others do to you.

Evans arrived in Bombay on December 9, 1877. He immediately set out to explore the city, and, in his next letter to Katie, was contemptuous of his fellow travellers.

Most English people stick to the ordinary humdrum of civilisation. The officers and ladies who came out with me spent to-day in visiting each other, loitering about the verandahs of the hotels, smoking and drinking, going to the club . . . I tried to get a party to go to Elephanta, and found five willing to join if it could be done early, before fashionable calling hour! That failed. Then I tried to get some to visit the Towers of Silence and the native town, and all said it was too nasty. So I took my own bent and went by myself.
My chief occasion for asking others was to save some expense in sharing a carriage, but it was far better alone than in ill-assorted company.

So he travelled alone, for three hours, and said he saw only one other European.

The Indians are better-looking than the negroes in the Southern States. Some of the women are really very pretty, and many as naked as the men, with only a loin cloth.
What clothes the poor had were very clean. I know extensive districts of London – Shoreditch, Hackney etc – where the majority of the people are far more dirty than the poor Hindus . . . So I am very favourably impressed at first.
I got out of the carriage in one place and mixed in a crowd of the poorest Hindus to know whether they smell as bad as it is

reported of them. I admit that they are not as sweet as desirable, but they are certainly far, very far more fragrant than a regiment of Irish militia. All the women have good figures with perfect grace in all their movements.

He made his way to the Towers of Silence, where the Parsees expose their dead to be devoured by vultures. With his usual thoroughness, he had obtained a letter of introduction to the priest in charge.

I had heard that it was a disgusting place and that you would see vultures with blood on their claws, heads etc . . . I saw many scores of vultures perched on the outer walls of the towers.
Many I saw flying up from within where they had been feeding. I examined them all carefully with the aid of my field glasses, and could see the details of the feathers, but I did not see a single drop of blood or any flesh on them. The man told me they were all very fat.

The priest spoke no English but sent for a young Parsee who was able to interpret Griff's many questions about the Zoroastrian teaching.

"Why don't you burn your bodies?"
"Because fire is sacred, and through it we worship God."
"Why don't you bury your bodies?"
"Because when a body is put in the ground it becomes mud. We must not defile Mother Earth."
"Vultures die and rot in the ground. Don't they defile the earth?"
"Yes, vultures become mud too, but our sacred books tell us to give our bodies to feed vultures."
"There are no vultures in England. What would you do with a dead Parsee in a cold country?"
"Our sacred books do not say anything about that. If we were so situated that we cannot do what the books tell us, we may do what we think best without sin."

After recording this dialogue for Katie, Griff comments:

I think that so far as there is any virtue in blind, unquestioning faith, a Parsee is as good as anyone.

During his hour in Bombay he also visited a Hindu burning ground:

I saw three fires, a body on each in different states of consumption. One was just commencing to roast, another was nearly all in ashes . . . I was allowed to stand on the wall within a few yards of the pyre; the win was blowing from me.

In his next letter from Bombay, a few days later, Griff wrote:

My dearest one, I have engaged a head servant . . . He is twenty years of age and can speak and write a little English and appears to be unusually intelligent. He is a Hindu. Many officers object to intelligent servants, but I take it as a recommendation if a man is good otherwise. I like this man's expression. I am glad he is young, that I may train him for myself. The officers of the 13th Hussars are greater swells than I am and faster in their ways, and a servant trained by them would have to unlearn a great deal to suit me.

During his time in India, fortune favoured Evans in that the sub-continent was benefitting from the long spell of relatively sound and peaceful administration which followed the Mutiny. The Government was making a serious, albeit parsimonious, attempt to stem the tide of famine and plague, and official opinion was beginning to favour the sort of field research which Griff had now been sent to undertake.

He had not expected the opportunity for any original work, and was thus the more pleased to learn, on arriving in Bombay, that he was to go at once to Sialkot to investigate a mysterious

114

disease which was making serious depredations among the army's horses.

Evans' posting to India had been made at the instigation of James Collins who had just succeeded John Wilkinson as the Queen's Principal Veterinary Surgeon. His brother, F F Collins, had been appointed Principal Veterinary Officer to the army in India. The brothers had met Evans at Curragh Camp and were aware of his exceptionally wide knowledge of medical and veterinary science, and knew that he was well-fitted for this special task.

On his long journey north, Griff stopped for two days at Agra, and there, the methodical scientist and rationalist that he was, revealed an emotional and near-mystical response to Eastern faith.

Agra. *December 19, 1877*
I went to see the Taj again last night by moonlight, and the full moon with the blue sky brought out new beauties which the day did not reveal.
I paid six shillings for lighting it up inside with blue lights to show the details within which are wonderfully beautiful. But to my mind, the most wonderful, the most beautiful within, is the echo.
I'll give you an extract from the local guide book which is not exaggerated. It is not possible to do justice to the echo:
"The chord of the seventh produces a very beautiful effect. You see, or seem to see, a lark you have been watching after it is swallowed up in the blue vault of heaven".
I laid myself on the tomb and sang all the notes, lying face upwards and pausing between each. The echo recedes upwards magically, and the effect of the seventh was most thrilling.
If I had called your name or the names of my children I believe I would have drowned myself in tears. I sang "Praise God from Whom all Blessings Flow" as well as I could, as a relief to my feelings which were getting the better of me, and to the great astonishment of the native guides. I listened for a long time afterwards to the slowly-receding echo until at last it was lost on high, yet a few whispering voices reached me again and again, telling me to be comforted for I felt lonely, the earth itself receding away. And I thought what comfort could I get on earth if all I love best were in tombs

. . . But the echo was so like a voice from spirit-land that it bade me live in hope, live for the living loved ones now!
No tomb ever made me wish to remain in it before. I was enchanted, like the Lotus Eaters. I felt as if Maria and Mother would appear to me there. I made the attendants be silent. The place was as still as any grave.
When I had, in imagination, passed the portals of life, and, in my longing for the dead, was almost seeing visions, a far greater longing came over me for the living ones. While my wife and children live, may God grant me life also, and pardon me if I sin in longing for the dead. So I thanked God most of all that he has given you to me to live for.
There can be no sorrow for me in life more than I can bear while you remain with me.

Griff's next letter tells Katie how he had met again a Baptist missionary named Gregson whom he first encountered in "The Great Eastern." Gregson took him along to the Baptist chapel in Agra where he found many men of the 60th Rifles whom he had known in Canada. They invited him to a temperance meeting, and he found it was a "flourishing regimental society, 170 members of good standing".

In Canada I used to provide open hospitality in my quarters for men who had a wish for somewhere to go besides drinking places, and I was delighted to find that here they have a capital room in barracks entirely at their disposal where they prepare tea and coffee for any men of the regiment, so that no-one has excuse to go to the canteen to drink. They also provide papers and books. My heart warmed to meet Sergeant Burns and the good men and true who used to come to my room in Canada. There were perhaps 150 there last night, the abundant fruit of small beginnings.
I spoke to them for some time from the depth of my heart.

During the next year at Sialkot Griff tried to sublimate his desire for Katie by an intense devotion to duty. In investigating the mysterious disease which was afflicting so many of the army's horses, he had to work under daunting difficulties.

116

You cannot imagine how trying it was. The glare, the intense heat, the stench, the lack of any other pair of hands, certainly did not make for fruitful research.*

Evans had been following with intense interest the researches of Pasteur into diseases caused by micro-organisms, and he must also have known of the recent achievement of the German bacteriologist, Koch, who, as recently as 1876, had isolated the bacillus of anthrax.

After weeks of concentrated toil, he firmly concluded that the many sick and dying horses at Sialkot were the victims of anthrax fever. He was the first man to diagnose the disease in India.

I floundered on, observing what I could. The symptoms varied extremely in each outbreak, according to the organs chiefly affected, respiratory or alimentary in different patients. I proved it to be anthrax fever by finding the specific bacilli in the living circulating blood of every patient.**

Scientifically, Evans was, of course, probing into very new territory. Bacteriology was still in its infancy, and in India little, if anything, was known about microbes – indeed it was not until that year (1878) that the word "microbe" was coined in Europe. Moreover, it was extremely difficult to detect the anthrax bacillus even with Evans' modern type of microscope.

However, as he later realised, he was on the verge of a much more significant discovery. During his observation of the blood of the diseased horses he had been puzzled by the increase in the number of white corpuscles. He felt that this activity was of significance and merited further investigation in good laboratory conditions. He had, in fact, been witnessing one's of nature's defensive mechanisms. Four years later, the Russian biologist Metchnikoff revealed the purpose of the white corpuscles now known as phagocytes, which have the protective function of engulfing or ingesting bacteria and other harmful particles.

*In a talk to Liverpool School of Tropical Medicine in 1917.
**Ibid.

117

Evans later said:

I officially reported what surprised me most, that the first change in the blood seen by the microscope was a great increase in the number of large, white corpuscles before I could see a bacillus. I expressed my conviction that the large, granular corpuscles had a very important relation to the bacilli, but I could not think what it was. I repeatedly emphasised my belief that it deserved special investigation.*

For the rest of his life, he was tantalised by his failure to recognise the function of the white corpuscles.

It is remarkable that Evans was able to carry out his investigation without any means of fixing and staining smears for microscopic observation. But in old age he remarked that having no stain for bacteria was not always a disadvantage, for "by close, continued observation of the living bacteria, especially in the bacilli, (we) noticed differences that few modern biologists are aware of."

His diagnosis of anthrax, although greeted with some scepticism, was accepted, but the authorities ignored his request for further investigation into the riddle of the white corpuscles.

During his field work, he ordered the deep burial of horses which had died of disease to prevent exhumation by starving outcasts. One day, however, some of these miserable people begged him to give them the carcase of a horse he had been examining, pleading that they would make it safe by roasting and adding quantities of pepper. In his letter to Katie, Griff said he could not deny their request, and warned the military police to look out for sickness, but fortunately none developed.

Griff sought to bring himself nearer to his wife by writing long letters running to forty or fifty closely-written pages which he posted weekly. And in May, 1878, he had an experience which gave him plenty to write about.

Sialkot, *May 5 1878*
My Katie! Is it a dream I have just waked out of? . . .

*In his address to the Liverpool School of Tropical Medicine, 1917.

Some of the servants who looked after the Evans family during their years in Madras.

The pony-trap (with Syce) which overturned on Griff at Ootacamund.

Sylk's Hotel, Ootacamund, where Katie gave birth to a much-wished-for son.

Griff's "dream" was, in fact, a visit to the durbar in Jammu arranged by the Maharajah of Kashmir to celebrate the marriage of his 14-year-old son to a bride aged nine. Evans had been invited among a party of officers and their ladies representing the Bengal army.

The durbar at Jammu – for long a centre of Indian culture – was on a scale similar to that given in honour of the Prince of Wales two years before. Then a palace was built by forced labour to house the Prince and his retinue, and it was here that Evans and his fellow guests were given rooms.

To describe his "glimpse into the Arabian nights", he wrote Katie a letter of more than 8,000 words. From his rising before dawn on a cool starry morning at Sialkot on the Thursday until his return on the Saturday evening, he savoured every moment. With six other officers he covered the journey to the Tawai River in a long, open carriage known as a "drag", with four horses and postillions, which the Maharajah had used to convey the Prince of Wales. Griff related that the Prince had ruined several horses which the battery at Sialkot had provided for him. He had forced them on . . .

. . . at a mad man's pace, getting up in his seat often, lifting his hat and shouting "Hurrah! Go on!" Several of the horses, the best of the battery, never recovered. Two died the next day and others had to be sold as worn out.

On reaching the Tawai, the party transferred to ten splendid elephants, "but the ladies preferred to cross the river by boat". Riding high in a howdah, Griff found the motion disagreeable, especially when mounting the quarter-mile of steps to the city.

When we arrived at the Prince of Wales' Palace which contains the finest rooms of any house in India, the party was served with a sumptious breakfast. Our number consisted of seven ladies, 25 officers and two civilians, besides four or five young children. One lady, having no child, brought her pet dog and was excluded from the durbar because she would not leave her dog in charge of anybody else, and dogs are not allowed at durbars. She felt aggrieved, but she was not the only unreasonable humanity among us.

In the afternoon Griff explored the palace and looked out at the magnificent views of the snow-covered mountains and the suffocating plain. And then . . .

A general in the Maharajah's army called to see us. He said that the durbar was going to be unusually grand, and that the best nautch girls had been brought for the occasion. One of us, a full colonel in the Bengal army, to my shame, asked the general what the entertainment would cost the Maharajah. The native general showed his better breeding by looking astonished, and then, in a tone of rebuke, replied, "I do not know what it will cost. Whatever it is, his Highness does it for the entertainment of his guests." And then turned and walked off.

The colonel showed his idiocy by laughing loudly. I felt inclined to kick him, and I took care to let our own general know it. Fancy anyone visiting a gentleman in England, and being feasted without stint, and entertained for three days, besides his conveyance, asking one of the host's chief servants what the entertainment would cost his master! It does appear sometimes that the notion of the transmigration of souls is not far wrong, and that this colonel had the soul of an ass in the body of a man.

There were also some among our number who went there purely for the sake of gluttony: unlimited champagne at every meal. Others thought it was their duty to find fault with everything. The Maharajah said it was time for rejoicing . . . and wished the pigs and other animals to have quietness to rejoice too.

At 7 p.m. we started a procession on elephants for the full-dress durbar. I find the greatest difficulty in conveying to you a faint notion of the scene. I could not possibly have imagined it.

Griff sent Katie several illustrations of the durbar, saying he had "a very good place, marked X, about the middle of the front row . . . I was sorry indeed you were not in the chair next to mine."

120

He was introduced to the Maharajah who (he explained) had been married twice, hated his first wife and was not fond of the sons she bore him, but was devoted to his second wife and her children, of whom the bridegroom was the eldest.

The King sat down. We did likewise. The dancing girls began to dance and sing. I was pleased they made no sign of impropriety as I heard they commonly do. But I was disappointed in the dancing and singing. There were two torch-bearers, one on each side of the dancing girls, to show them off more distinctly. I had heard of the beauty of the Kashmir women, but never expected to find one nearly as beautiful as several I saw, really charming faces, beautifully sculptured and pure withal, but they spoil their figures by squatting so much.

I won't attempt to describe the fireworks, which are a hobby of the Maharajah. After that we were dismissed, and marched home accompanied by torch-bearers. We returned to the Prince of Wales Palace as hungry as wolves.

Next day, the British guests were escorted round the Maharajah's palace "spellbound by the view".

One of the most beautiful landscapes I ever saw. There was a wonderful calmness of beauty . . . We were all whispering as if we felt ourselves in the presence of the supernatural. I wished I might gaze at that view for ever. If I could by some magic transport it to Wales . . . nowhere could be more conducive to everlasting sleep.

Then back to the palace for more singing and dancing:

I examined the nautch girls through my glasses and saw many pretty ones among them. They soon found out I was admiring them and expressed their willingness to be admired by smiling most sweetly and trying to look serious at me, by turns . . .

One of them had remarkably good features and expression of eyes. She was a well-bred Kashmirite. I remarked to the company: "That girl is beautiful now, but she would be much more beautiful without that ornament in her nose." I had hardly spoken before she took the ornament off. She made no other intimation that she understood what I said. I went up to her and found she had lived three years at Sialkot where she learned to understand a little English but she can't speak any. She gave the ornament to me for inspection. I told her she was ten times more beautiful without it. She smiled charmingly.

Griff explained to Katie (who may not, perhaps, have been quite so enthusiastically interested in nautch girls as her husband seemed to be) that they did not often marry because Hindus chose young brides who were reconciled to restrictions to which the nautch girls, having tasted freedom, would not submit. However, they had many admirers among married men with whom they might co-habit.

I do not know if that is any more immoral than the custom of marrying a stranger to please one's parents, and becoming his slave, or being one of several such wives.

That night, the celebrations reached their climax with the customary honouring of the small bridegroom prince:

. . . the poor boy so weighted by a heavy velvet and gold-embroidered robe, massive solid gold crown, and thick gold veil hanging from the crown over the face, that he could hardly walk.

Then followed the presentation of gold and silver gifts.

I was told that every officer and man in the (Maharajah's) army has to give the prince a month's pay. If that is true it is very unjust.

Back in Sialkot, Evans resumed his daily routine, spending much of his leisure, when not writing to Katie, in studying Hindustani. His *munshi* was . . .

a very godly man. Although Towyn folk would regard him as a heathen, he is more Christian than most Christians, comparable indeed to Uncle Rees, the best type of good Christian.

He also studied the Hindu religion, "asking questions, checking with the answers I received down in Agra, comparing the religion of the Hindu ruling majority with the Muslim working peasants." He said he respected the Hindus for recognising symbols as symbols; their image-worship, he said, had been much misrepresented.

He found some uglier aspects of life in Sialkot. In the open market he was disturbed to see children being sold by their parents. Yearling boys fetched tenpence to a shilling in equivalent Indian currency and girls less. Sometimes, girls were given away.

Evans' reputation for thoroughness and veterinary skill now brought reward. Mr J J Collins informed him that he was to proceed at once to Calcutta and that he was to be promoted to the rank of inspecting veterinary surgeon, his new rank to take effect the following February (1879); meanwhile he was to undertake the duties in an acting capacity.

The journey to Calcutta took three nights and two days by train in fierce heat. On arrival he posted a letter to Katie containing sheaves of Sanskrit poems. He comments:

You say that Towyn is becoming a very bad place. You only echo a common cry everywhere. The Hindus and the Mohammedans complain of exactly the same thing.

After this, Katie received no letters for several weeks and later said this was one of the most agonising periods of her married life. She feared he had been sent to fight in the Second Afghan War*. The fact was, he was desperately ill. In August 1878 he was

*Britain had declared war on Amir Shere Ali who was intriguing with Russia. The British were advancing by the Khyber, Kurran and Bolan passes.

stricken of a fever, and, once again lay near to death. Fortunately, he had told a Welsh cousin in Calcutta that he was coming to the city. The cousin took him to his home and engaged a nurse for him. To prevent Katie from worrying, Griff had asked that she should not be informed of his illness.

Calcutta *October 19 1878*.
My Katie ... The doctor at first misunderstood my case completely, but he did me little harm. My own diagnosis proved nearer true; for several days I thought I would probably die ... The prospect of leaving you and the children was terrible. I cannot believe there is worse terror in death than what I went through. I believe that if I had not been removed to Cousin's house with a good nurse, I could not have survived.

Griff told Katie not to worry any more about the Afghan War. He would not be going there. He would begin his round of inspections towards the end of November. Although the roads were notorious for robbers and very lonely ...

... you need not be afraid on my account. They dare not kill me in the Queen's service, but they will try to rob me if they think they can succeed. I shall certainly not spare to shoot them if they try!
The last words I spoke last night as I went to rest were: I thank God for my dear Katie. I was soon after fast asleep.
I dreamed that something of me incorporeal visited you and found you in bed. It was dark but I could see you as if a light emanated from yourself as a glow-worm. I said "All the heart of my soul as well as my body sends love to you."

Griff then awoke to find himself looking through an open window into an Indian dawn ...

Dawn in her wedding garments. Venus the morning star twinkling all over with joy as she sank into the arms of her

124

beloved Eros. Such was the dream and such the reality. I
wish I were a poet that I might make both immortal, and I
wish you were here with me to see the morning birth.

Doubtless Katie shared his wish, but she would rather be compared with something other than a glow-worm! His letter went
on:

Don't you wish that we were all again as we were at the
Curragh. I shall never see my charming, bonny, *little* children again, who used to walk up my body and stand on my
shoulders. They will be my *big* children when I see them
next, quite different beings. The loss to me of this period is
more than I can estimate.

During his convalescence he often walked on the roof of his
cousin's house, looking down on the streets of Calcutta.

Hardly any Europeans go out walking here, they all take
horse or carriage exercise. Calcutta is a very fashionable and
dressy place, being the seat of the Indian Government in
winter months. I see the men in tall hats and kid gloves and
black frock coats as if they were in London . . . Temperature
in my room in a good shade has been 88 every day of this
week.
I can't describe the women's dress. I am determined to keep
out of society here, no satisfaction can be got out of it. I do
not feel in the least lonely except for you and the children
because I have plenty to divert my mind: reading rooms, a
very good museum of natural history and geology . . .

He described how the "untouchables", who swept his room in
cousin's house, sought to maintain human dignity by addressing
each other with high-sounding titles:

"Will the greatness of your majesty condescend to lend me

your broom?"

"The Sahib calls for your high majesty to go quickly to empty the chamber vessel."

"The Sahib is very angry because your highness has not swept the floor of his room."

In his new role as inspecting veterinary officer (with the rank of major), Evans was responsible for the vast area of the Ganges basin. Little of his circuit could be covered by rail; much of his journeying was comparable to travel in Europe during the Middle Ages. When he was not on the back of a mule or borne in a dak-gharry, he rode in a rattling coach "worse than any railway I have been on, taking eight hours to cover fifty miles and in danger from robbers all the way." Yet, between November 1878 and February 1879, he visited Meerut, Delhi, Agra, Morar, Allahabad, Fyzabad, Futtehpore, Kurali, Lucknow and Benares. After which he said:

I have seen more of Bengal and the North-West Provinces than most people who have been here the greater part of their lives.

From Morar he wrote:

This is the most detested station I have ever been to. About 50 men and seven officers died of cholera here last summer.

His letters home showed that he was still feeling the after-effects of his serious illness. Following a very long journey to Lucknow, he went to bed at midnight in what was considered the best hotel. In his exhausted condition he underwent a night of horror he could not explain.

27 November 1878
Now I will tell you a remarkable event . . . very ghost-like and for all I know it was a ghost if there be one.

126

I awoke with a slight chill and heard some movement, and was convinced that somebody was walking past my bed . . . like an immensely heavy dog.

I spoke but received no answer. I listened again, and heard the sound much more distinct as it went all round my bed. I spoke again in English and in Hindustani. I shouted for my servant but got no reply. I could not reach the matches. My pistol and sword were out of reach. I could stand it no longer and got out of bed and determined to make the best fight I could. While I was searching for my matches, the sound of rubbing and scratching increased, and sounds of heavy, panting breathing were distinct. The moment the match lighted, all the sound ceased and I found my door closed with no-one in the room but myself. My servant was fast asleep outside the entrance door, lying across the path as the custom is.

Next day, the landlord of the hotel said that he had complaints of that room before, and the ever-curious Griff discovered that before the British took Oudh some twenty-five years previously, the pleasure-loving Ali Khan, King of Oudh, had allocated the building to the successive commanders in chief of his army; and the unused rooms surrounding that in which Griff slept had been part of the harem.

I was less afraid of ghosts than of bad men, so I made no objection to sleep there the following night, with my revolver, sword and umbrella within convenient reach . . .

Katie's reply to this, some weeks later, was an irrepressible comment that neither dog, man, nor ghost would have stood much chance against a gun, sword *and* umbrella!

Griff's second night in the "haunted" room was scarcely less disturbing. He dreamed that his sister Maria appeared before him "accompanied by the odour of death".

I understood her to say that I had promised to pay for the education of her boys, and I replied: "I have no recollection

127

of making any promise of that sort." She looked distressed and said very slowly, "You do not understand." And she gradually dissolved away.

The dream seems to reflect a sense of guilt, a feeling in Griff that he should have done more to help his sister and shown more concern for her three boys.*

In December, Griff looked back on the year 1878 and wrote to Katie that he was glad she did not know at the time how ill he was in Calcutta. He wondered how he had managed to struggle through so much work when his body was so weak.

There is in my nature, while I am free from actual pain, the element of continued perseverence. I take real pleasure in overcoming difficulties. That is my instinct. I am not in any way "brilliant", and never was, but a plodding tortoise that sometimes passes the sleeping hare.

Katie tried to raise his spirits by common sense and gentle teasing.

My dear Griff,
I am much interested in your speculations about the future life. They are so heterodox and original – many people would say blasphemous. Anyhow, shocking to imagine that dear Maria regrets in heaven that she did not take better care of her body, and that you can conceive of nothing in heaven to soften the bitterness of parting with your loved ones here!
Why, according to orthodox ideas, you would be so absorbed in contemplating the marks of nails in Christ's hands and the gash in his side and in singing his praises, that you would not recognise me, even if I sat by your side!
It must necessarily be all speculation about the future life –

*Maria's boys were being well looked after by a kindly Welsh girl whom John Jones later married, inheriting the farm of the girl's parents, near Barmouth.

unless we believe in the Spiritualists. There is hardly a hint of it in the Bible. It is the feeling of "something accomplished, something done" gives us the greatest satisfaction here; and unless we change our nature, it will be impossible for us to be happy in heaven feeling that there is nothing more for us to do . . .

She went on to give him news of the children, which she knew he would read with delight.

At teatime, Erie put a cushion on her chair to make herself sit tall, and announced, "If any strangers come in now, they'll think I am a woman." But Wynona chided her: "For shame, Erie! That is as bad as *saying* an untruth, because you are trying to deceive!"
We have nearly read "The Water Babies", and you would be amused to hear Erie and Towena playing; sometimes they pretend to be caddises. Erie is very fastidious about trifles. Clothes must sit exactly right. It may be a virtue that she can do things for herself, but very trying on cold mornings!

She told him how, when the children were in bed, she loved to sit with her hands folded, doing absolutely nothing for a while, to the astonishment of an industrious neighbour.

Mrs Smith is never happy sitting down to talk without some work in her hands. She thinks me very lazy because I enjoy perfect idleness. She thinks I ought to take some active part in Sunday School or visit the poor or do something outside my home . . . I am very glad you think it is the noblest work I can have to educate my own children. I miss you dreadfully in that work . . . Your absence, Griff dear, has indeed made me feel how bound up my happiness is in you, and I feel grateful, oh so grateful, for your love . . .

CHAPTER THIRTEEN

Ordeal in Bengal

Evans spent a lonely Christmas staying in a hotel in Lucknow. In the morning, he visited places connected with the Indian Mutiny. In the afternoon, he wrote a long letter to Katie telling her what happened in Cawnpore some twenty years before.

He told her that when, on the previous Monday, he stayed at the Railway Hotel in Cawnpore, he had discovered to his astonishment that the proprietor, a retired army man, was a native of Katie's village, Llanfaircaereinion; he was the son of "Edward Lee who farmed Mynafon", and remembered Katie's father well.

At the time of the Mutiny Lee was a sergeant in the first detachment of the 53rd Highland Regiment which marched into Cawnpore after the massacre of the British men, women and children who had capitulated there to the rebel Nana Sahib on his false promise of a safe transit in boats to Allahabad. In his letter to Katie, Griff repeated the first-hand account of the slaughter which Lee gave him:

> I was taken by Mr Lee first to the site of the small entrenchment thrown up by our people, and saw the well from which they had to procure water at risk of life . . . After capitulation, they were led to the water close to a small Hindu temple that still remains. Nana allowed some to go in the boats, but a considerable number of the women were picked out and retained, their husbands, fathers, brothers and sweethearts also being allowed to remain with them. Then the word was given to massacre all those not so reserved.
>
> Those reserved were taken to the assembly rooms, men and women separated, the men killed. Some of the women were given that day to Nana's friends, including the two Miss Wheelers, daughters of the massacred British general. One of them still lives; she is the mother of seven children, and

she refused several offers of release. The last offer was made within the present year by her brother. But no European has been allowed to see her. She says she can't part with her children. The other Miss Wheeler managed to kill her captor, and escaped to drown herself in the well of Cawnpore.

Next day, when Nana learned that Havelock was near with his little band – he did not know how small it was – he ordered all the surviving women and children to be killed, but had difficulty in finding executioners. His soldiers refused to do it. When he ordered them to fire, they fired into the air. Then he got three villainous Mahommedan butchers (by trade so) and gave them sharp swords to go into the rooms, and told them not to spare a single person of any age.

There were a great many women and children, and it took the three men nearly the whole day to kill them. When Sergeant Lee arrived with Havelock's brigade, the ladies remained as the murderers had left them. In some rooms the pools of blood were ankle deep, and mothers and children still clasped each other in the convulsive grasps of death. Several women *enceinte* were ripped open, unborn babies on the floor by them. The limbs of many had been severed.

There was a quartermaster who, when he saw Nana coming with his soldiers carrying white children on the points of bayonets – shot first his own two children, then his wife and lastly himself to save torture . . . There were many bodies in the well close by, but Lee says they were *not* put in by the natives, as some claim. The natives, except those of lower caste, would not touch the dead, fearing defilement, and the lowest caste would not without order and payment by higher authority. No order was issued to dispose of the dead. They were left for carrion if our soldiers had not arrived in time. Lee is quite sure, from the evidence of natives, that the bodies found in the well were those of women like Miss Wheeler, who drowned themselves rather than submit to the villains.

Early in January 1879, Evans received a letter from Mr F F Collins requesting him to undertake single-handed the duties of the annual casting committee, first at Nowgong and then at far-distant Sangor at the mouth of the Hugli River in Bengal. The casting committee's job was to decide which military horses should be disposed of as being below standard. Surplus military horses were much in demand, and the committee, while ensuring that the army's high equestrian standard was maintained, had to prevent first class animals from being dishonestly branded as below required efficiency, thus frustrating the ruse, commonly adopted by cavalry officers, of enabling their friends to buy cheap horses. Normally, the committee consisted of three senior officers, but Mr Collins explained that the two colonels, who would have joined him to form the committee, were unable to make the long journey to Nowgong, so he must act alone.

Although doubtless flattered by this evidence of trust in his integrity, Evans was certainly dismayed by the remainder of Collins' letter which told him that, following his promotion to inspecting veterinary surgeon, he must stay in India for a further five years. He made no attempt to conceal his dismay from Katie:

> Five years is more than I can bear to entertain now. The experience of the past year has not tended to reconcile me to live apart from you.

However, Griff's gloom was tempered by the hope that within the next year or so he might become the Principal Veterinary Surgeon in India.

> I stand a very good chance of succeeding Collins in Simla; and, in that event, I am in hopes of bringing you there, too, if we can manage the welfare of the little ones.

His next letter was written from Nowgong in wild Assam:

> Nowgong is only a military station of recent date with no native or other town, placed there to awe the native independent rajahs. The country between Bonda and Nowgong is most interesting. There is much wild land inhabited by

132

jackals, wolves and panthers which feed on the beautiful deer ... Serpents are also very common. The wife of the colonel commanding the cavalry regiment there heard a hissing near her when she was in her bath, and, turning round, saw a large cobra in the room. Last week a Mrs W saw a bushy tail of some animal in her bedroom when she was getting up, and, moving a box, she saw it was a huge jackal in hiding.

At Nowgong, the colonel and other senior officers were not too pleased when Acting IVS Evans presented his credentials. It was unprecedented for a veterinary officer, who had not even been officially gazetted as IVS, to undertake alone the work of a casting committee. The officers suggested that, since the two colonels, who should have accompanied Griff, could not be present, two of the senior Nowgong officers should take their place. Evans, however, was not to be brow-beaten.

I told them I saw no reason to depart from the instructions I have received from the Government of India and that I would commence my duties tomorrow morning. No doubt the Government of India knew what it was doing.

Knowing that Katie was an admirer of George Eliot, he passed on some gossip given him by the husband of the Nowgong lady who found a jackal in her room:

Mrs W tells me that the lieutenant in the next bungalow is a cousin of George Eliot. Before Mr W knew of the relationship, he remarked to him that it was reported of Miss Evans that she had "gone wrong" with a gentleman.
The cousin was very indignant and said there was no foundation for it. Mr W also says that a Mr Poyser, veterinary surgeon of the 6th Dragoons, claimed that his grandmother was the veritable Mrs Poyser of "Adam Bede". I was very surprised to hear that George Eliot is nearly sixty years of

133

age, and was married not more than four years ago to the late Mr Lewes.*

On arriving at Futtehpore, on the way to his second casting mission, at Sangor, he wrote:

Here I am again, just returned from a jolting in an almost springless dakgharry for 28 hours, halting for only one hour at a dak bungalow yesterday evening.

At times, the poor ponies were augmented by oxen or camels. Once, twenty men had to be enlisted to haul the dakgharry when it became stuck at one a.m. in deep dust going uphill, and Evans and his servant had to put their shoulders to the wheel.

I had no refreshing sleep and arrived too late for the train from Futtehpore. I shall proceed tomorrow by rail via Allahabad to Sangor, that is, two days and two nights by dhooli-dak from the railway. That is, a conveyance on the shoulders of men. There is no other means of going there except on foot.

Soon afterwards, Evans' servant succumbed to a fever and he, too, had to be carried. Twelve men (six turnabout) carried Griff and six others carried his servant.

We travelled at night for two nights, resting the intervening day. The big dhooli that bore me is so heavy that I could only carry it for a few yards at a time, taking one end alone, but these twelve men, three at each end at a time, changing often but hardly stopping, carried me with my bedding and

*Gossip travelled more slowly in those pre-tabloid days! George Eliot had "gone wrong" many years before: it was in 1854 that she decided to live with Mr Lewes. When Griff wrote this letter, Mr Lewes had been dead for only a few weeks (he died November 28, 1878). George Eliot died two years later, in December 1880, six months after marrying Mr J W Cross. The Poyser link sounds very improbable.

The ayahs who looked after Katie's babies at Ootacamund.

Travelling in India.

The Dawk Gharry.

Evans jolted over thousands of Indian miles in
almost springless vehicles of this kind.

Indian street scene in the late 1870's—a snap from Griff's Indian scrapbook.

small luggage for 37 miles at a stretch in 13 hours. They are all Hindus, vegetarian and teetotal, walking barefoot, with hardly any clothing, humming a song all the time ... The road is through wild country, hilly and stony and very dusty so that by morning I felt choked with dirt.

Sangor is by far the prettiest place I have seen in India, yet it is far from healthy. It is a great place for bees. I saw several swarms, and, near the falls, saw a marble tomb of an English gentleman who was attacked by a swarm which drove him for refuge to the river, in which he drowned himself.

This would be a place of great resort if it were in Europe or America, where great improvements would be made by Art. Here all is left to nature. I was never more convinced than today that nature in all her phases can be improved by man, from cultivating the Garden of Eden to trimming a man's beard.

He saw many pilgrims along the way, and at one point came upon two fakirs squatting beside their beds of spikes.

I gave them a few coppers to make them communicative. They stretched themselves out on the spikes which did not injure their skin but hurt the muscles, and caused the limbs to be stiff and sore. One was old, the other about 25. Both were unwashed, hair unshorn and matted, unclothed, and all over covered with ash and dirt ... I asked the young man why he used a spiked bed, and he replied, "I do it for the sake of my stomach." I suppose the pain diverts his mind from hunger, or maybe it was to make people think he was a holy man and give him food and money.

A few days later, when Griff was travelling by train to Lucknow, a Roman Catholic priest entered his compartment. He was an Italian, who spoke good English and "reminded me of pictures I had seen of Wycliff." He thought that Evans must be a Roman Catholic, when they discussed the fundamentals of Catholic belief, but was quickly corrected.

I told him I belonged to no sect but was in fellowship and

communion with all who served God as Christ did. I protested emphatically against every sect that ordains priests, whether it be the sect of the Pope of Rome, or the Greek Church, or the Episcopal Church of England, or the Presbyter of Scotland, or the Brahmans in India, or the Buddhists in China, or the Moslems of Asia. I protested against priestcraft in all its forms as being contrary to the gospel of Jesus Christ.

He was rather astonished. But he took it all in good part and said he did not know how to argue with me because I recognised no published creed.

When the pair arrived at Lucknow – perhaps to the great relief of the priest – they shook hands warmly.

The old man bore me no ill will, though when I expressed the hope that after this life we might meet again in Heaven, he looked rather doubtful, but smiled and said farewell.

In his next letter, from Allahabad, Griff asks:

Did I tell you that the Pundit has informed the Maharajah of Kashmir that the soul of his late father now inhabits a fish, and a royal proclamation has been made strictly to forbid any fish being caught in Kashmir?

When his tour took him to the fertile farming lands of Fyzabad, he expressed concern about the rapid growth of population:

I am coming to think it is evil rather than good for us to supply food to them in famine times since they will not emigrate, and persist in multiplying their numbers to a greater extent than their land can feed them.

At the same time he wrote to his children, his letter reflecting

136

his deep sympathy for an injured goose:

> The goose had broken her leg and she was being attacked by
> a carrion crow. The gander was in despair, and the poor
> goose resigned herself to torment. The two were constantly
> talking to each other. I never heard geese making the same
> sounds before. The tones of their voices were so distressing
> that I was miserable for hours afterwards. Their lamenta-
> tions haunted me and I do not exaggerate in the least. The
> voice of the goose came from her chest and had the tone of
> resignation and despair . . . The gander's voice came from
> his throat and nose, and was a kind of suppressed sob, a soft
> tremulous voice of grief, but when he succeeded in driving
> the crow further off than usual, he would open his wings,
> give a cry of exultation, run forwards, put his face close to
> the face of the goose, and speak some accents cheerfully.
> Soon they would be sorrowing again.
> Since birds show such affection for each other, we must not
> be unkind to them. I am sure that most animals have kinder
> hearts than we credit them with, and they have more intelli-
> gence too, which it would be worth while studying.

At about this time – January, 1879 – Griff received a distressing
letter from his sister Eliza, telling him that his ageing father was
being harassed by a creditor for the £300 he still owed under the
disastrous guarantee given many years before, which had already
swallowed up the family fortunes. Old Evan, it seems, could have
settled the debt by selling Tŷ Mawr and his 23 acres, but had
refused a fair price. In his weekly letter to Katie, Griff gave vent to
his exasperation:

> Eliza says if she had £300 she would pay it for father to wipe
> off "the disgrace" . . . I can't see any disgrace. It is his
> misfortune, an error of judgment, not in principle. I am
> truly grieved but I do not see any reason for me to take up
> the burden which has crushed father. I, as well as Eliza and
> Maria, gave up all that Grandmother left us – £3,000 – in
> order to pay father's debts, – debts not contracted for any-
> thing on our account. I have always refused to go beyond

that, and I am not disposed now to make any heartless generosity to satisfy the sentiment of the public, who are quite ignorant of what my sisters and I voluntarily and cheerfully signed away when we thought it would be of use to our parents. Moreover, I have no money to give . . .

This letter was brought over to Katie as she sat in Gwalia Villa watching by the deathbed of her great-aunt, Catherine Jones, for whom she had a deep affection ("Dear aunt Gwalia, left over from the eighteenth century.") When she answered Griff, it was gently but with realism. His father, she said, had only a few more years, at most. "We must do all we can to make those years bearable." Meanwhile, Griff had gone to Calcutta, where he met Meyrick and evidently told him of his father's plight. And thus it was the staunch Meyrick who came to the rescue of the family. He begged to be allowed to make a loan of the £300, and when Griff refused his offer, he dispatched the money to Katie, and by the same post three tiny Indian shawls for the little girls. Griff later told his wife that she might accept the money, "but we must pay Meyrick interest."

On the occasion of his meeting with Meyrick in Calcutta, Griff had just been gazetted as Inspecting Veterinary Surgeon and was congratulated by the generous Meyrick, who himself still awaited promotion after ten gruelling years organising the breeding of horses in the Punjab.

Katie wrote to Griff expressing much sympathy with Mr Meyrick and wished he could come to Towyn to meet a certain Miss Hitchcock, who, she was sure, would make him an excellent wife. Meanwhile, she said, "everyone in Towyn was delighted to see the three miniature Indian ladies being piloted around the streets" in Mr Meyrick's shawls.

During the next few months, Griff's letters to his wife showed signs of strain and introspection. He seemed to be living in the past and filled page after page with nostalgic memories of his childhood at Tŷ Mawr.

Then, in June, he sent Katie a secret letter in which, it seems, he laid bare his soul. He asked her to destroy the enclosed letter, but she kept the outer letter which accompanied it. This gives no clue to the nature of the secret which troubled his mind and had to be confided to his wife.

I wrote the enclosed the day after I sent you my last letter, and it is a great relief to my mind to submit it to you. A good woman's instinct is far better than reason to guide me out of such darkness as I have been in for some time past. "Valley of the shadow of death" it may truly be called. The enclosed will explain how and why we got into it. For years I have trusted to guide myself and you through it safely. Having failed, I resign myself completely to you for leadership to guide us both to light and freedom and assured safety again. I yield to you both rein and whip and whether it is necessary for you to lead or drive successfully through.

I make no reserve whatever in this case but rely upon you with that confidence which I wish you to place in me in other cases.

From this enigmatic statement it must be inferred that Griff had something which he felt he must confess or confide. And when, several weeks later, Katie's reply arrived, he destroyed it, but, plainly, was at once uplifted. He wrote immediately to say that she had made him very happy.

The Hindus have no conception of love between husband and wife as we understand it.

He rushed out to buy her two gifts, one to mark their wedding anniversary, on October 26, the other to celebrate the tenth anniversary of their engagement, which was not until the following April. The latter gift was the most exotic bold necklace he could find. It was perhaps too barbaric and chunky for Katie's little neck. The centrepiece was a locket engraved with a little Indian image. Inside, Griff wrote in fine script:

In memory of Foundation days, April 1st 1869 to October 26, 1870.

And, in his letter, he wrote:

139

These gifts are in token of the happiness of our marriage. You must always associate them in your mind with the 1st April. The intercurrent of true happiness has ever flowed like a stream of life between us, from one to the other, ever since that day. That current has never ceased to swell whatever obstacles have met it. The greater the obstacles the stronger the current increased until the misunderstandings had to be removed. Our prospects in each other were never clearer and brighter than now. And however dark the future may be, regarding the immediate prospect of bodily reunion, my soul will ever find its rest in you. And God will bring us together again. Be sure that I shall never cease to be your own devoted

Cariad anwyl   *Griff.*

In her reply, Katie said:

I shall associate whatever you send with 1st April as well as 26 October. Nothing has interrupted our happiness since our marriage until within the last six months, and that interruption I now look upon as really an increase of our happiness. Griff bach anwyl, whatever happens to either of us, we are sure we shall be happy together again sometime.

What interrupted their happiness "within the last six months" remains a secret.

The previous autumn Griff had sent Katie a photograph of a Miss Burton which, for some reason, he thought would interest her. And in her next letter, Katie referred to it light-heartedly:

I know how beautiful she is. I believe you would have fallen in love with her, too, if your heart had not been already filled with the perfection of all human excellence in my person.

Years later, Katie told her youngest daughter, Mair, who was also to suffer separation from a husband out East, that it was hard for a man, parted from his wife for long periods, to sublimate his physical desires. "The great thing," she said, "is to be sure you keep his love."

Touched by his gifts, Katie sent her husband some money to "buy a little dog as a gift from me, to ease your loneliness." But Griff said he would not have a dog. "I shall get fond of it, and I can't take it to England and then I would fret." He recalled his two dogs, Terra and Snap, which he had when a boy, and said he would ever be grateful to them.

> I have never met in man better examples of faithfulness, forgiveness of injuries, doing good for evil and a great desire of pleasing with cheerfulness . . . whence came their attributes but from the Creator? If the dog is so good, how good God must be!

In her reply Katie had a gentle tilt at his frequent nostalgic reminiscences about Towyn:

> Do you think, Griff dear, that it will be possible for you to enjoy any of the many excursions of Heaven unless they bear some resemblance to Towyn? I never knew or read of anyone so tenacious of old associations as you. You cling to everything and everybody for whom you have at any time felt any degree of affection.
> I am very glad your health is so much better.

Griff now became friendly with Keshub Chunder Sen, the Indian religious reformer, who opposed child marriage and persuaded the Government to pass a special marriage act for Brahmins. In 1878, however, he allowed his own young daughter to marry a Hindu prince and Katie said he was a humbug. Griff replied that Keshub Sen sincerely believed in the ideal of educating Indian women but found that in practice it did not work out, and he did not want it for his own daughter. Missionaries, he continued, had not always done Indian girls a service by educating them, and he describes two such girls who had passed the normal marrying age for Indian virgins.

141

It seems cruel to advance them too soon. These girls are looked upon as useless appendages, abnormal virgins. One is the private tutor of Keshub Sen's daughter, and the other is principal of the Ladies' School. I saw her yesterday. I never saw such a timid hare of a woman. She is now 27 years of age and Keshub Sen told me she is by far the most highly educated woman in India. She wants a husband, yet there is no intelligent non-idolator native of a suitable age who wants a wife.

But if Griff was dubious about enlightenment for Indian girls, he undoubtedly approved of it in his wife:

Katie's independence of mind had led her into trouble with the minister of her chapel at Towyn, and she was threatened with excommunication. She wrote to her husband:

Last night I had a call from Mr Symonds, our minister. He had become alarmed by my circulating the autobiography of Harriet Martineau . . . "It is the most dangerous book of the age," he said, though he allowed he had not read it. He abused Charles Kingsley and all the men of that school, and said they could not possibly be good men . . .

I told him all my doubts and difficulties, which of course horrified him, and the end of it was he told me I must not go to the Seiat* any more, while I am in "such a dreadful state of mind." He told me I was in the grasp of Satan, and further from Christ than anyone in the Chapel, and that my guilt was immeasurable after having had the advantage of being brought up with such a good man as Uncle Rees even to allow a doubt to enter my mind.

I am not sorry to be broken off. He did what he thought was his duty and he is thoroughly good, though the narrowest of the narrow . . .

It is plain that when Griff heard of this he almost danced with glee.

*Chapel Meeting

My own dearest Katie,

Your last letter was the best tonic medicine I have had for a long while. The idea of your having been excommunicated from the Corff for heresy is very refreshing! . . . I am sorry for the Corff* but you are free, and in a more healthy atmosphere. My sorrow is for the pain it has given, I suppose, to good Uncle Rees . . .

You will probably be visited by a deputation from the Seiat, but not one of them will be able to understand any of your arguments . . .

In your case, as a woman, and with your natural dislike of publicity, perhaps it is better for you to retire quietly, but I think if you felt capable of standing the pressure and worry, you would have done more good by refusing to retire as long as possible, to force a discussion of your doubts, first in the Seiat at Towyn, next in public papers, and in the Seiat Fisol **

I would back you up, to make the whole of Wales discuss your doubts. So that has been the result of your reading H.Martineau! Who did you lend the book to?

The last thing Katie wanted, as a mother and home-maker and loving niece to her elderly relatives, was to be the subject of conversation for the whole of Wales! She replied:

I am quite amused, my dear Griff, with the pugilistic tone of your letter. You seem prepared for a stand-up fight with the Corff. I am sure, and I thought so from the first, that it would be better for *others* for me not to retire from the chapel without having my heresy discussed. I believe there is a great deal of latent scepticism amongst the younger people in Wales, and they only want someone to speak out for them. But *I* don't feel equal to the "row". It would make me quite ill to become a Marked Woman. It would pain Uncle too much for me to be talked about, as I should be. If you were here, I should not mind. I have no doubt that the whole affair will ooze out, by and by, but it won't make such a sensation like a public excommunication.

*Body of the Chapel
**Monthly Meeting

143

She then recounts what she said to Mr Symonds, the minister, and Griff was doubtless proud of his five-feet-two Katie standing up to her accuser.

> I told Mr Symonds that I did not believe the infallibility of the Bible, nor in Eternal Punishment, and that I doubted the divinity of Christ. Curiously, he did not ask me anything about the Atonement. When he told me I was entirely in the grip of Satan, I replied that amongst other things I had given up a belief in a personal Devil and he said: "I daresay, indeed, Mrs Evans! That is one of the delusions of Satan these days, that people may not recognise the doubt as *coming from him!*" . . .
> Mrs Jones Neptune Villa came to beg of me very kindly not to unsettle Miss Jones Gwylfynw's mind . . . It would make Miss Jones' life at home so very miserable if she took an independent path . . .
> I did not lend H.Martineau's autobiography to anyone but Mrs Jones Neptune Villa and the Gwylfynw people. They joined me in sending for it.
> I hope indeed we can protect our children from all that may hinder them in searching after truth. The dogma of eternal punishment will have disappeared almost entirely soon, and when people cease to think they will be punished everlastingly for doubting certain things, they will be free to question them . . .

Uncle Rees was in failing health, and at the end of August Aunt Rees asked her niece to escort him to Great Malvern to take the waters. This was a welcome change of scene for Katie.

> It is great fun to go up the (Malvern) hills on Saturdays because an excursion brings a lot of boys and girls, and there is no end of courting going on. Uncle was much impressed by your cousin Griffith of Aberystwyth's economical habits. He saw him on the station at Towyn smoking some tobacco rolled up in paper, instead of a cigar.

The Malvern waters did not help the saintly Uncle Rees, who

144

died a few weeks later, leaving Katie to cope with her querulous old aunt. Her earnest little daughter Erie was sensitive to the atmosphere.

Erie told me last night when going to bed: "I don't think I can live. I am more unhappy now then I have ever been. Uncle dead, and Father in India. The girls at school think the end of the world is near, because so many are dying."

In addition to all her other cares, Katie was now beset with the dread that her husband would be "murdered by the Afghans". Not surprisingly, she felt the need of a tonic, and her doctor recommended a daily glass of port wine.

It might have been wiser to have omitted this item of news from her weekly letter. Her husband's reaction to it came as a thunderclap. A cablegram from Dr Evans to Mrs Evans arrived at Towyn Post Office:

DRINK NO ALCOHOL

This message must have been flashed round the little town within minutes. Of course there had been gossip about Mrs Evans' sudden absence from chapel. Now this! Poor Mrs Evans had taken to the bottle, just like her father! And her dear Uncle scarcely in his grave!

It was as well that nature had endowed Katie with a sense of humour. The tactlessness of Griff's cable had to be spelled out to him, and he was contrite, but adamant, that she must not touch alcohol even as a tonic. Plenty of sleep, good steak and fresh air: these were what she needed.

This same letter contained such splendid news that she readily forgave him his unfortunate cable. First, he was not to go to the Afghan War. Secondly, he was temporarily promoted to take Collins' place as head of the Army Veterary Service in India. And last and best, Katie could come out to join him.

Mr F F Collins had summoned Evans to Simla, the summer seat

145

of Government, and announced that he himself would be going to the Afghan War and meanwhile Evans was to take his place in Simla. He suggested that now Mrs Evans could be brought out to India.

It was Griff's ambition to succeed Collins, and his selection as unofficial deputy seemed a promising augury. He proposed to Katie that she should join him in about a year – in the autumn of 1880, avoiding the hot weather and providing time to make arrangements for the children. He rented "the last house out of Simla on the road to Tibet", and took up his duties immediately.

He delighted in his new environment: the fresh mountain air, the forests of pine and deodar, the meadows where in spring hyacinth and asphodel, celandine and rhododendron grew. He stood on Mount Jakhu to see the sunrise over the eternal Himalayan snows, and wandered in the hills to visit the marriage markets. When he described to Katie the pure gold trinkets hanging from the noses of women, she teased him in her reply: Would he like to see her with a ring in her nose when she came out to India?

His letters became more affectionate and playful: he began to sign himself "Griffy." He regretted that he was absent from his children in their budding years:

When I return the time of blossoming will have arrived. I have always been fond of budding children, and more fond of my own buds than of the flowers of others – except you, Katie.

He adds the not very comforting remark:

When you come to India, you will be able to understand and feel the grief I have now in the loss of my children's childhood.

And to the children he wrote ponderously:

Your dear Mother will come to me next year . . . And as I

shall have borne three years without her for you, so you will bear years without her for me. You know I am more fond of, and love your Mother more than it is possible to imagine . . . and when we all meet again, won't we be a happy family!

On Christmas Day, 1879, he enclosed with his letter to Katie a sketch of himself sitting alone warming his hands at a small log fire. And in red ink he printed below it:

FATHER CHRISTMAS WITHOUT HIS CHILDREN, ALONE ON THE HIMALAYA.

He took his duties as acting Principal Veterinary Surgeon very seriously; there is more than a hint of the "new broom." He told his wife that his most disagreeable duty was to discipline the veterinary surgeons at Simla. Some of them were lazing about and shirking work.

I warned them, but when they took no notice I could not wrangle with them, but decided to hand them up sharp to the commander in chief for discipline . . . The veterinary surgeon of the 13th Hussars will I fear lose his commission. But it will be a gain to the Service.

Like countless other wives of Victorian empire builders, Katie was torn between husband and children. To uproot herself, abandon her little girls, part from her friends and prepare to live perhaps for years in a strange, far land – it was all so much more difficult for her than Griff seemed to imagine. Some army friends allayed her fears by recommending a school at Woolwich where, they said, her little girls would be well looked after and happy. It was one of the many schools which grew like mushrooms all over London for the left-behind children of parents abroad. Only when she returned after five years in India did Katie discover the truth, that the Woolwich school was sparse in learning and meagre with food, and little better than the establishment later described by Kipling in his story "Baa Baa Black Sheep". All the

147

other children, except two small boys, had been gradually removed.

She arranged that during the holidays the girls should stay with Griff's sister, Eliza Dedwydd, in Wales, and that Gwenddydd, Griff's warm-hearted niece should take them to and from school. Then there was the problem of Aunt Rees. She became almost demented when she heard that Katie, her only close relative, was going to desert her. "Who will bury me?" she wailed. Griff offered little comfort.

I trust poor Auntie will live long, and that in her ripe old age she may be laid in an "elegant and comfortable coffin" as I saw advertised in Montreal. I am very sorry to learn she has become so unreasonable . . . By this post I send her a letter on the subject of your coming out which I hope will help her to be reconciled.

He advised Katie not to argue with Aunt Rees, but just to go on quietly with her preparations for the voyage, and not to come until the end of September because of the great heat in the Red Sea. When he was told that "poor auntie" would not see reason, but had received his letter in utter silence, and never referred to it to Katie, while she in turn obeyed his instructions and did not discuss her plans with her aunt, Griff in his new exuberance was able to see the comic side.

Simla. *April 12 1880*
I expect if you had neither cariad nor children, and lived with *her,* you would both become pillars of ice – not salt! . . . Farewell, my love, for another week. You are the constant delight of my heart.
Your own sweetheart

Griffy

Katie asked him if she might send his love to Mrs Jones of Woolwich with whom she was in correspondence over the question of schools, and "Griffy" replied jauntily that she might send any message she liked, but although he had a "sincere respect" for

Mrs Jones, he suffered from a "physical antagonism" to her.

> If I were alone with her on an island, and had never known
> you, I should never have the least desire to kiss her or even
> touch her hand . . .
> Your passage to India from Southampton to Bombay or
> Madras will cost £68 besides the fee you will be expected to
> give the stewardess, ten shillings or a pound according to the
> trouble you give her . . .
> I shall send you full directions for your journey and voyage
> by and by.

Apprehensive about emerging from Towyn into the relative
sophistication of British India, Katie had asked for practical hints
on how to be a sahib's wife, and the advice Griff gave included
this:

> Don't ornament your under-linen too much because the
> native wash-men beat them against stones . . . Don't call
> "Badminton" parties "Babington". Did *I* make that mistake?

Katie's letters were now taking on a more skittish tone. She
always loved to tease her serious husband, and it is difficult to
believe, after the port-wine incident, that the following – written
after a visit to Eliza – was not meant to be wilfully provocative.

> I felt quite tipsy after Eliza persuaded me to drink some
> home-made elder wine, because the breezes of Portmadoc
> had chilled me.

By return came the inevitable rebuke.

> Simla, *May 2 1880*
> Katie bach anwyl,
>   I am *not* sorry you got so tipsy on elder wine though I *am*

vexed Eliza gave it to you, and that she makes it so strong for domestic use. She is in danger of giving her children, and perhaps herself, a taste for strong drink. Alcohol got by fermenting elder is as bad as any other. I hope it will be a warning to you not to be tempted again. If you should feel cold like that, take a good draught of hot water and some lemon juice. And sit in a bath *with hot water between your thighs*.

In red ink he emphasised:

You must make Eliza promise solemnly that she will not let one of our children taste her elder wine, or let them have other alcohol drink of any kind under any circumstances whatsoever when they are in her charge.
On no condition must you let them go to her house, other than this, before or after you leave.

Perhaps a little ruffled by this pompous tone, Katie wrote, after her next visit to her sister in law at Portmadoc:

Eliza showed me another likeness of you taken in a very imposing attitude, sitting on a chair with a paper in one hand, and the other hand pointing to it, and your face looking round for an appreciative audience. I have no doubt your father and mother were very proud of it. I forgot to bring it away with me, but will have it again to keep with the one in the locket. They may be useful, like Pollie-say-Pork, if ever you show a disposition to forget the "rock from whence you were hewn."
Your own loving

Katie

In her next letter, Katie said that the children's teacher in Towyn had taken to making her class lie down on the floor to get good posture, but at the same time they had to read their school books. Griff was appalled and wrote indignantly:

Tell Mrs Williams plainly from me that I must seek another

school for our children if she insists on making them lie on their backs to learn lessons. It is injurious to read in that position, both to the eyes and the chest and to the circulation.

His letters were at this time reflecting the intensity of his physical desire for his wife. She was in his thoughts day and night.

I have been dreaming about you every night this week . . . One day I arrived home and seemed to see you and the children meeting me! I ran forward with my arms open to embrace you . . .

Conscious that he found it easier to bare his heart in letters than in speech, he warned her:

You must not be disappointed if I appear at first as cool as you used to think me in 1869. You must not misinterpret me as you did then, because I was not more "off my head".
Your most loving cariad and devoted husband.

When Katie wrote that Mr Symonds, the minister who had expelled her from chapel, had lost his wife, Griff sent her two pages of the sin of causing a wife to have too many children, a practice not commonly regarded as a sin at that time.

Husbands are often morally guilty of murdering their wives by not denying themselves the pleasure of sexual passion.

This was the last letter Katie received before she sailed in September. She resigned herself to becoming "like a Mahomet's coffin suspended"* on the high seas between children and husband.

*Annette Beveridge's phrase, quoted by her son, the late Lord Beveridge in "India Called Them."

It was just as well that it was too late to let her know of a sudden change of circumstances that would have caused her the utmost distress. Griff was ordered to the North West Frontier.

CHAPTER FOURTEEN

Pioneer on the North West Frontier

Towards the end of August, 1880, Collins returned to Simla in haste from the North West Frontier. He told Evans that he wished him to leave as soon as possible to investigate an outbreak of the dreaded disease of surra among the horses of the British Punjab Force.

The military commanders, he said, were alarmed by the severity of the outbreak. A considerable number of horses had already been lost and hundreds more were in their death throes. At one small station alone, Jutta, the 3rd Punjab Cavalry had lost 77 animals. The rapid spread of the disease represented at least a minor crisis in the conduct of the Second Afghan War. Like the rest of the army, the British Punjab Force depended on horses; without adequate transport their very survival could be at stake.

Accordingly, the army had requested the Government to take immediate action towards discovering the cause of the disease and, as they optimistically hoped, a cure for it. The Government's "immediate action" was to pass on the army's request to their Principal Veterinary Surgeon, Mr Collins, and now the responsibility was squarely his.

For Collins, who was due to retire the following year, it was a daunting burden. Surra, a wasting disease, had been the cause of terrible depredations; it could wipe out entire studs.* Veterinary surgeons knew virtually nothing about the cause or the way in which it was spread. They were baffled, powerless.

Inevitably, Collins turned for help to his deputy, Griffith Evans, who was the most competent and experienced man on his staff and had shown his mettle in diagnosing anthrax during the

---

*One Indian nabob had recently lost his entire stud of 300 horses as a result of the disease.

serious outbreak of horse disease two years before. Well aware that Mrs Evans was due to arrive at Calcutta in mid-November, Collins said he regretted the inconvenience which his sudden request might cause to Evans' personal arrangements, but in an emergency such as this the demands of the service must take priority. However, he hoped Evans might complete the investigation in time to meet his wife. But it is doubtful whether Collins in his heart really expected Evans to find a quick answer to the problem, or, indeed, that he would find one at all.

Collins told him he would be based at Dera Ismail Khan, on attachment to the Assistant Adjutant General, Punjab Force, and from there he would be able to carry out investigations at all the stations along the frontier.

The British press had described the frontier as "the most dangerous area in the world", therefore Collins assured Evans that he would be provided with an adequate military escort as he travelled from post to post.

When Evans said that he would require permission to slaughter a number of horses for post-mortem examination, Collins agreed that there was no reason why he should not dispose of sick horses which were doomed to die anyway. But when Evans insisted that it would be necessary, in order to observe surra in all its stages, to transfer the disease to selected healthy animals and ultimately to make post-mortem examination of them also, Collins felt that this was going too far. Never, he said, could he sanction the sacrifice of healthy horses. When so many were succumbing to the disease, the army could not afford unnecessary loss. There would be an outcry at the very idea. In that case, Griff said firmly, he could not undertake a thorough investigation. He asked permission to appeal to higher authority which Collins grudgingly gave. In the end Griff won his point:

Strong objections were made to giving the authorisation I requested. The question was ultimately referred to the Lieutenant Governor of the Punjab personally, and after some further cross-fire he decided entirely in my favour.

Meanwhile, Evans was pursuing his practical preparations.

I asked to be furnished with all the reports made on surra by

154

surgeons, human and veterinary. After reading them I was of the opinion that it was due to some parasite in the blood, though this was not suggested by anybody else.*

He put his theory to two of the Government's principal scientists in Simla, Dr Timothy Lewis, Special Assistant to the Sanitary Commission for India, who also worked for the Army Medical Department, and Dr D D Cunningham, the Surgeon-General and Director-General of Hospitals.

Both of them greeted his views with extreme scepticism. Evans had for some time enjoyed a friendly relationship with Lewis, a fellow Welshman, and must have been taken aback by his blunt rejection of the parasite theory. Experiments with rats had convinced Lewis, evidently beyond argument, that any parasite existing in the blood of animals must be harmless.

In the middle of September, Evans left Simla for the desert town of Dera Ismail Khan, on the banks of the Indus River. He arrived on the evening of Saturday, 18th, and next day wrote to his children:

I arrived here all right but exceedingly tired after crossing this horrid desert from which I have not yet recovered. I find this heat very great, day and night.
Your dear mother will have left you before this reaches you. I hope she will have a fair passage and that I may be able to meet her in Calcutta.
I shall have to go about a great deal to out-of-the-way places on the frontier. I have to be escorted from place to place by a troop of cavalry to protect me from the murderous Afghans who are always on the look out for unprotected travellers.

At the military station, Evans was warmly welcomed by the CO, Major Gowan, who told him that there was, unfortunately, no lack of sick horses with which to experiment. He also made

*These and further extracts later in this chapter are from a paper which Dr Evans wrote for the Liverpool School of Tropical Medicine in 1917 describing his investigation. It was published in the Annals of Tropical Medicine in July, 1918. The other principal source of quotation is Evans' "Report on Surra Disease".

available several healthy horses which were lame or otherwise no longer fit for service.

Evans went to work and quickly confirmed that the disease afflicting the horses was surra. When he came to write his report – which was to make veterinary history – he began by explaining the name and nature of the sickness.

The name surra is used by the natives to denote anything "sur-gia" – gone rotten – and is given to this disease because a withering or falling-off in condition is a marked feature of its progress. In England we speak of the "rot" in sheep, and "decay" and "consumption" in man, to denote affections characterised by wasting during life. This disease is quite new to science but . . . it is not new to reality, for it has been only too well known to the natives of Dera Ismail Khan for several generations.

Notwithstanding Lewis' dismissal of his idea, he began work on the assumption that the disease was caused by a parasite in the blood.

I had to work with the microscope for many hours a day out of doors at the sick lines, or else in a stable when the thermometer was 82 degrees in a "cool" bungalow; the sun pouring down its rays through a cloudless sky upon the surrounding bare ground. Very few investigators know what that means.

Moreover, the flies were an additional torment, for when they crowded upon the stage of my microscope, disturbing the vision, soiling the lenses and swarming on my face, it was not possible to fan them off without beating and shaking the microscope. The blood which I was examining or else the tissues of the body at post-mortem examination attracted them, and thus, much of my energy was expended in self-control under that provocation.

He took dozens of specimens, comparing the blood of sick horses with that of healthy animals. The evidence revealed by his microscope was dramatic: the blood from the sick horses was teeming with parasites.

Evans was so elated by his first observations that he went hurrying into the mess to find Dr Haig, the cavalry unit's medical officer, and begged him to come down to the sick lines. He put a drop of blood under the microscope and invited Haig to see for himself, adding, "See, it's alive with microbes!"* The doctor, after studying the specimen, said that the parasites were quite new to him; he could not imagine what they were. He was astonished by their violent activity, and, because of the ferocious onslaught they were making on the red corpuscles, he suggested that Evans should give them the name "Ferox". He asked what their significance could be, and Evans said he inclined to the belief that they were pathogenic. During the next few days Evans worked with much intensity on the theory that these parasites were in fact the cause of surra.

He injected into four healthy horses blood from diseased animals, either into their stomachs or under their skin. They all sickened, and, within six days, their blood swarmed with the surra microbes.

I communicated the disease from a horse to a dog and a bitch, likewise by sub-cutaneous injection of the blood and by the stomach. They sickened, and the microbe appeared in the blood. The bitch had a young pup that became affected with the disease by sucking her. I could not account for it otherwise, though I did not find the microbe in her milk. It was necessary to make further experiments carefully to decide that question.

Evans then made post-mortem examination of organs taken from diseased horses in order to discover whether the microbes were confined only to the blood.

The weather was exceedingly hot, but I had plenty of ice in large felted baskets to preserve the organs while I examined

*The word "microbe" had taken the place of "micro-organism" in 1878 at the suggestion of the French scientist, Dr Sedillot.

157

them . . . I found no casts in the urine. I examined the dung carefully, morning and evening, for worms et cetera, and found nothing abnormal . . .

At this stage, Evans appears to have decided to his own satisfaction that the disease was caused by parasites which had in some way invaded the bloodstream of the suffering animals, and later he based his report on this conviction. Scientific history has named Evans as the first man to discover what is now know as a pathogenic trypanosome* (his variety being named *Trypanosoma evansi*). The essence of his achievement was to recognise that protozoan parasites in the blood are capable of causing disease. This was contrary to the firmly-held belief, not only of his colleagues, Lewis and Cunningham, but of most of their scientific contemporaries, that such parasites were harmless.

The disease which Evans was investigating is now known as trypanosomiasis or, more commonly, sleeping sickness in man, or nagana or surra when it attacks cattle or horses. His discovery triggered off important developments in the identification of disease-producing organisms, and these, in turn, had profoundly significant influence on the opening up of territories, especially in Africa, where the disease had caused and continued to cause the loss of untold numbers of human and animal lives.

Evans, who described himself as having witnessed "the early dawn of present-day pathogenesis", made it clear in the paper he wrote in 1917 for the Liverpool School of Tropical Medicine, that his discovery was not entirely a fortuitous incident. Microscopy had been his hobby since his earliest student days, and throughout he had a particular interest in the analysis of blood.

I had kept myself informed of Pasteur's investigations and discoveries of pathogenic bacteria and was deeply impressed with the conviction that a new door was opening for great developments in medical science.

Having decided that the parasites were the cause of the disease,

*A pathogenic trypanosome is a disease-producing, unicellular, flagellate protozoon, a parasite in the blood of humans or animals. Protozoa are the lowest and simplest form of animal life. The flagellates have a long cilium or whip-like appendage used in locomotion.

Evans had to resolve the problem of how the microbes got into the horses' blood in the first place. Were they, he wondered, in the water which the horses drank?

He tried to contaminate water by pouring diseased blood into it, but these tests were negative: there was no sign of the microbes in the water after it had stood for 24 hours.

Then he hit upon what was, indeed, a vital clue to the mystery. The natives at Dera Ismail Khan had long believed that the lethal disease was caused by a type of fly they knew as "bhura dhang". He remembered from his boyhood a similar belief by the old Welsh folk living around the undrained marshes of Towyn, who always declared that it was the mosquitoes, dancing over the marsh, which gave them the ague.

The so-called bhura dhang was a blood-sucking fly, the size of a small bee. Was it conceivable that this insect could transfer the microbe of surra from horse to horse by means of its proboscis? It was a flash of inspiration and there were several items of evidence to justify the thought. But he could not carry out tests: autumn had come and the flies had suddenly become scarce.

In his report he drew a thick line down the margin beside the following paragraph to emphasise its importance:

It is not improbable that these flies, so exceedingly troublesome at Jutta and other outposts, which bite horses so that the blood streams down the legs as if it had been squirted on, – it is not improbable that they do convey the disease from one horse to another by inoculation. It is a fact that the disease does spread mostly at those posts where horses are closely packed and the flies are in greatest numbers, but those are the posts, also, where the drinking water is worst, so that it is exceedingly difficult to form a true opinion upon the subject without further experiments.
However, the indications at present are that the horses affected with surra should be kept at a distance from other horses during the season when those flies are common. They were becoming scarce in the early part of October . . .
I do not know yet what is their scientific name. They are very large, of a brown colour, and common in many parts of India. The natives call them "bhura dhang" which means a "great needle-like sting".
There is a common opinion prevailing among the natives of

Dera Ismail Khan district, that this fly is the cause of the disease. I think the fly may sometimes propagate the disease by inoculation and thus be an item among the causes to account for the spread of the disease, more at some posts and in some years than others, though the diseases would exist independently of them.

When the horses stand close together, the fly is able to go from one horse to the other before the blood about its mouth is dry; whereas if it had to travel some distance through the dry air in the hot sun, perhaps the virus of the blood would be destroyed.

So it was the swarms of flies which had exasperated Evans as he sweated over his microscope – or, at any rate, the "bhura dhang" among them – which he now regarded as primary suspects in the spreading of surra. His hypothesis was eventually to be proved remarkably accurate. But the suggestion that the parasites were transferred from one horse to another by blood-sucking flies was ignored at the time, and Evans has been given but scant credit for it since.

It was not until fifteen years later that David Bruce isolated the similar trypanosome which causes sleeping sickness and. further, recognised the tsetse fly as being responsible for conveying it to the human body. And, as W D Foster records in his "History of Parasitology" (Livingstone, 1965), the first person actually to demonstrate the mechanism by which surra was transmitted was Leonard Rogers, who, in 1899, showed that *Trypanosoma evansi* was in fact transferred by the bite of tabanid flies: that was nineteen years after Evans had pointed to the "bhura dhang" as the probable carrier.

In early October, Griff had to tear himself away from this part of his investigation, in which he had become deeply absorbed, in order to carry out an inspection of the eight frontier posts.

At each one he collected a considerable amount of data which he incorporated into his report. He examined both sick and healthy horses, made a comparative analysis of the incidence of the disease, studied the terrain and analysed the water. He covered the eight posts in as many gruelling days.

He wrote to his children:

I rode along the frontier on horses and camels with a strong escort of cavalry, and in one pass I had an infantry escort to guard the upper crest of the hills. There was no road anywhere.

The people of the hills often make raids on the farmers and villagers below, stealing their cattle, their women and children. Sometimes they attack in a large force. I saw one town, four or five times as large as Towyn, burnt down by them lately, and the people either killed or driven away ruined.

People in England never hear about these raids or "little wars" which are carried out by the independent tribes of Afghanistan and have no relation to the "big war" you have heard so much about lately.

I hope your dear mother is all right now, on her way out.

Evans returned to Simla on October 19, almost five weeks after his departure. He brought back with him various specimens, including two of the blood-sucking flies, and, most important, the pup which carried within itself live parasites. He at once began to compile his "Report on Surra Disease", which he determined to complete in time for him to meet Katie in Calcutta. But he was too meticulous a man to skimp his report. Half a century later, Dr R F Montgomerie, FRCVS, writing in the "Veterinary Record", described it as a "masterpiece".

He called on his friend, Dr Timothy Lewis, to tell him of his findings which he thought might prove of great consequence; and he took with him the pup he had infected with surra. This pup, he believed, would be valuable evidence to corroborate his theories, because . . .

I wished to learn what I could by passing the disease on from him to other animals . . . to learn whether the disease is really communicable by milk only from mother to sucking pup, and whether the microbe is to be found in the milk. Moreover, I was anxious to show the living, active microbe to other medical men, particularly to Dr Cunningham and Dr Timothy Lewis.

To Evans' astonishment and chagrin, Dr Lewis dismissed his conclusions with contemptuous disbelief. He could not deny the presence of the microbe, but he would not accept that any such microbe, found in the blood of a living animal, could cause disease: any disease, he argued, must have developed as a result of chemical change. Lewis was himself a parasitologist of repute, but he was convinced that the parasite which he had detected in the blood of brown rats, which was later to be given his name – *Trypanosoma lewisi* – although similar to that found by Evans in the blood of horses, was not in any way damaging to the blood of the rats. When invited to examine a sample of the blood taken from the pup, he said:

> These microbes are morphologically the same as those I found in the rats; perhaps with some slight difference. I cannot accept that the similar parasites in the blood of horses are pathogenic. They couldn't possibly be the cause of surra.

Evans protested that Dr Lewis was ignoring the evidence, and reminded him that the pup had been infected with the same microbes which swarmed in the blood of the sick horses. He asked:

> If these parasites are not pathogenic, why is it that they do not exist in the healthy horses I examined? When the microbe is introduced into the blood of a healthy horse, that horse sickens and is plainly suffering from surra.

Lewis said that was not conclusive. The microbe, he argued, could be there merely as a result of the horse having contracted surra.

"But what of the pup?" Evans repeated that it had been infected with the same parasite and now was showing signs of surra.

"That pup," replied Lewis, "is merely suffering from the common distemper of dogs!"

This was an insult to Dr Evans' intelligence, but, in fairness to Lewis, it must be recognized that at that time there was only one trypanosome known to science and that was the one which he himself had found to be non-pathogenic in the blood of rats. He could scarcely contemplate the upheaval in the approach to disease if parasites of this kind were proved to be pathogenic.

At the army HQ in Simla, Evans' medical colleagues saw nothing but obsessive obstinacy in the bloodshot eyes of the veterinary inspector, and obviously thought that the gruelling month he had just spent at Dera, staring into a microscope, must have overheated his brain. They did not see a pioneer; they saw a crank.

It was ironic that Dr Lewis was much more excited by another, but quite minor, discovery which Evans had made. In examining some camels suffering from surra in the lines of the 4th Sikhs in the Punjab, Evans had traced in their blood what he recognised as a previously unknown filaria.*

He took the specimen back to Lewis, who was a specialist in filaria and Lewis enthusiastically agreed that it was an unknown strain and was at pains to ensure that Evans was given the credit for its discovery. It was later named *Filaria evansi*.

Dr Evans' "Report on Surra Disease" was submitted to the Governor of the Punjab on November 13. Katie was due in Calcutta the following week.

Collins decided that Dr Evans needed a rest and a change of scene. He suggested to him that after meeting his wife, when her ship docked, he should take her with him up to Assam and spend two or three months investigating, at his own pace, an outbreak of disease – not surra – amongst the horses in the army stations there. In the New Year they could return to Calcutta, the Government's winter location.

Griff left his valuable infected pup in the care of Lewis. He trusted him to keep the animal under observation and perhaps make further tests which he hoped would confirm his theories.

---

*A filaria is a nematode, i.e. a round worm or a thread worm, introduced into the camel's blood by mosquitoes.

CHAPTER FIFTEEN

Banishment

In capital letters, heavily underlined, Griff wrote in his diary:

NOVEMBER 19 1880 KATIE ARRIVED AT CALCUTTA ABOUT NOON

Katie described her arrival in a letter to her daughter Erie:

> We reached Calcutta on Friday, and long before we got into harbour I saw dear Father there waiting for me. I recognised his walk and knew him long before he knew me. We were obliged to look at each other from a distance a long time before the ship could be brought near enough for him to come aboard, which was very tantalising. I was more glad than I can tell you to see him again. We are staying in Calcutta a week and then we are going a very long way . . .

The three children she had left behind were never long out of her thoughts. They were staying with their aunt Eliza until it was time for them to go to boarding school. She had written them cheerful letters throughout the voyage:

> I felt the heat less because I did not wear stays . . . The donkeys which carried passengers into Suez Town were called Mrs Langtry, Lord Beaconsfield, Sir Roger Tichborne . . .
> In Ceylon I bought three combs of Tortoise shell for you and your sisters. Towena must not wear hers for another year . . .

I am sure you will be quite happy at Borth. You might learn to speak Welsh quite well. Ask Taid to speak Welsh to you.

After her three years' separation from her husband, Katie was still young-looking and pretty. She was now thirty-six, and Griff was forty-five, but looked older. His face bore the marks of his hard years in India, and, in maturity, he had become more authoritative, dogmatic and impatient.

Calcutta, Katie decided, was noisy and claustrophobic. She was glad they were soon to leave for Assam.

In Assam they stayed mostly at Silchar and Shillong. Katie was surprised by the size of their first residence in Silchar. "So many doors and windows!" she exclaimed in one of her frequent letters to the children.

It is called the Circuit House, a building for Government officials. There is a regiment of native soldiers stationed here with British officers. Altogether there are 22 Europeans. Four of them are married. Father and I went round to call on the four ladies as it is the custom in India for newcomers to make the first call.

Did Auntie remember to bring the eiderdown from Rhianfa?

Griff soon diagnosed the disease which had broken out among the horses in Assam. It was anthrax fever. His duties were light, and evidently he was enjoying his second honeymoon. Katie said Christmas was the most unusual she had ever known. They toured the tea estates and were warmly welcomed wherever they went. Griff took her on two excursions to the Khasi Hills where she was carried in a joppa, a small chair with a hood. She drew a little picture of it in her next letter:

I was very glad to have had the second trip to the hills. At Shillong I saw what I have never seen before except in pictures of Eastern customs – the famous Khasi dancing and tribal rites.

165

It thrilled her to see elephants, buffaloes and flying foxes, and she quailed at the jackals and the vultures hovering overhead.

One day we made a special excursion to the Presbyterian mission, hoping to meet our old Welsh friends, the Reverend and Mrs John Roberts. Father went on to the verandah of their bungalow, which appeared deserted and called out in his most stentorian tones: "A OES CYMRO YMA?"* and out came our two friends, their arms stretched in welcome . . .

Her letters show how eagerly she awaited news of her children:

Wynona said you wouldn't write because you had nothing to say, Towena. Just think what you would say to us if you were in the room with us, and then write that.

Their father added this message:

My own darlings. Remember always that your dear mother and I are of the same mind and heart, so the letters she writes to you come as much from my heart in love to you as if I wrote them with my own hand. Wynona says she got the ring in the plum pudding on Christmas Day. I hope you didn't forget to wish all the *poor* children had as much good pudding as you had and gave some bread and cake to Robin goch [Robin redbreast] when he called to wish you a happy new year.

He exhorted the girls not to play with certain of the Borth-y-Gêst children "who now have many bad words". He thanked them for their "very good letters", and promised them a list of their spelling mistakes.

Katie must have been deeply touched by a note from Aunt Rees

*"Is there a Welshman around here?"

Katie with Griff in the garden at Brynkynallt, Bangor.

Griff in his study. His gesture of deafness—cupping his ear with his hand—was characteristic.

Left: Ellen: A girl of spirit and a born nurse.

Below: Griff in the drawing room at Brynkynallt.

saying that, when the children visited her in Towyn, Erie had begged to sleep alone in her mother's bed so that they "might seem closer together".

Griff's escape from the cares and conflicts of official life was soon to be ended. At the end of February 1881, the Evanses set off for Calcutta; their honeymoon was over – and Katie was once again pregnant.

Before leaving Assam, Dr Evans had been made aware that his report had not been greeted with any sort of acclaim. He received a frigidly official note, written on behalf of the Governor General of the Punjab, acknowledging his report and adding:

> His Honour will not at present offer any remarks on this interesting report, but he extremely regrets to observe that no cure for surra has been discovered.

The problem of finding a cure for the various forms of trypanosomiasis, sleeping sickness, nagana or surra, was to baffle scientists for generations to come – but the Governor General of the Punjab extremely regretted that Evans had not been able to find the answer in four weeks! And clearly his theories about parasites and blood-sucking flies were not the sort of "immediate action" which the army had expected.

As soon as he arrived in Calcutta, Evans was told by Collins that his views were not regarded as acceptable and that the official opinion was that he had "mistaken effect for cause".

Evans pointed out that he had anticipated this objection and believed he had disposed of it in a paragraph in his report (which contained an obvious dig at Lewis and Cunningham):

> The question is whether the presence of the parasite is the cause of the disease, or whether the disease is the cause of the appearance of the parasites . . .
> There are some eminent pathologists in India who deny the parasite origin of specific blood-diseases; they say the cause of all such diseases from smallpox to anthrax fever is not any organic spore or germ or parasite of any kind, but it is some purely chemical agent which has never been discovered and that these organisms develop at once in blood which has

been so chemically altered.

What cut Dr Evans to the quick was to find that Dr Lewis had made no effort whatever to pursue research on the pup which had been left in his care. Griff had staked his hopes on this little animal providing additional evidence in confirmation of his findings. He at once went to see Dr Lewis and Dr Cunningham, and later wrote this account of what must have been a very painful interview:

I told him (Lewis) I had been particularly wishful to utilise the pup to inoculate another bitch and prove under more careful conditions whether the surra parasite did pass via the lactial glands to sucking pups. It was of the greatest importance to determine the ways in which a pathogenic germ is transferred.

But Lewis did not agree that the germ was pathogenic. He said:

I am positive that the parasite is no more pathogenic in this dog than those similar parasites which I found in rats.

Dr Evans then asked:

How do you know that the rats *were* healthy? How long did you keep them under observation? Did you take their temperature? A *casual* observer might not have thought that this pup was ill when I left him with you. But *I* knew because of my long experience of dogs and because of my close observations. Probably an expert on rat pathology would say that the rats which you thought were healthy were in truth not healthy at all.

Evans does not say how Dr Lewis reacted to this contemptuous reflection on his professional thoroughness, but adds:

It was useless to go on talking. He and Surgeon-General Cunningham remained obdurate. They seemed to think I had a bee in my bonnet.

In a later account, Evans said he was content to wait. "I knew that I should be proved right." He claimed that he felt no bitterness towards Lewis, but he thought he had been guilty of a breach of trust in not making laboratory tests on the pup which, on his return from Assam, Griff found to be "in a pitiful state."
But scepticism, as Griff himself well knew, is an essential ingredient of scientific progress, and with hindsight, in 1917, he acknowledged that he had put forward his theories long before Koch "published his classical postulates", and added, "I was groping in the dark with psychological rushlights only, impelled by strong scientific faith."

And even so distinguished and open-minded an authority as Sir William Osler admitted (in 1887) that on first seeing his friend Evans' "Report on Surra" he had been incredulous, and could not believe that "flagellating organisms should occur in the blood let alone that they should be pathogenic."

Now that the Indian Government's Sanitary Department had come down so heavily against Dr Evans' theories, his chief, Mr Collins, seems to have been persuaded that his deputy did, indeed, have a bee in his bonnet, and that all he had succeeded in doing in the Punjab was to kill off a number of healthy horses and camels. One suspects that Collins was under pressure to get rid of Evans, and he would have good reason to feel that it was undesirable to keep so strong-minded and argumentative a man in abrasive contact with the scientific establishment in Calcutta. Evans was clearly no longer acceptable to succeed Collins as the Indian Government's Principal Veterinary Surgeon – which he would almost certainly have been had he not been called upon to solve the problem of surra.

Accordingly, he was informed that he was to be posted to faraway Madras as the Inspecting Veterinary Surgeon for the Madras Presidency. It was an important post, but Evans can have had no illusions about why he was being sent there. It was virtually banishment.

Mr Collins offered him one crumb of comfort: a letter from the Secretariat of the Indian Government hoping that IVS Evans would be "induced as opportunity offers to prosecute his researches in regard to the disease, surra, which has proved so destructive and baffling." In view of the lack of opportunities for research that were available to him in his new post, the hope was more pious than real.

Over half a century later, Dr R F Montgomerie wrote in the "Veterinary Record":

So far as India was concerned at that time, Evans might as well never have visited Dera Ismail Khan, never have seen a case of surra, never have discovered *Trypanosoma evansi*.

When Evans came to place on record the reasoning which brought him to regard microbes as pathogenic rather than as forms developing in blood diseased through some chemical change, his light shone with real brilliance. Logic – yes! the purest of pure thinking set out what now seems an unanswerable case. Yet officially he was hounded for his views. He was regarded as a crank. He was forthwith sent from Bengal.

His report was consigned to the Government archives – and forgotten. However, early this century, its yellowing pages were discovered by a group of German scientists who were studying sleeping sickness in India. One of them commented to William Roberts, a Welsh cotton planter:* "This man Evans seems to have done all our work for us thirty years ago!"

A few years later, the report was destroyed, and when in the 1920's Sir Frederick Smith was writing his "History of the Royal Army Veterinary Corps", he was told that not only the report but all also the relevant correspondence (which doubtless included the written views of Dr Lewis and Dr Cunningham) "must have been sacrificed along with obsolete files."

Fortunately, at Evans' request, Collins had sent a copy of the report on surra to "The Veterinary Journal" in London, and the editor, George Fleming, published it; although in such a way as seriously to diminish its value. It was broken up into six instalments spread over a year. Moreover, as Evans later complained, Fleming had deleted some parts of it.

*later Sir William Roberts of Khanewal.

"Nobody will take any notice of it," Griff wrote. "I wish I had sent it to the 'British Medical Journal' instead."

And certainly in England nobody seemed to take much notice of the report. But the British veterinary profession was informed of the way in which Dr Evans had been treated by the Indian Government, and was angered. Sir Frederick Smith records: *

Considerable feeling was created in the veterinary service by the attitude of the Sanitary Commissioner [Dr Lewis], and "The Veterinary Journal", in its issue of 1881, hit back hard. The "Army and Navy Gazette" also took up the case and said that the Military Department of the Government of India had aggravated their offence by publishing a further criticism of Evans' discovery, this time from the pen of the editor of the "Indian Agriculturalist", a gentleman who admitted he knew nothing of the subject, but forwarded a preparation which could cure animals in any stage of the disorder!

It was clear that Evans had a friend in London who was championing his cause, and there is little doubt about his identity: it was his staunch friend Meyrick, who had now been posted back to Woolwich. Before leaving India, James Meyrick had a farewell meeting with Griff and Katie and was told about the fate of the report. The indignant Meyrick carried the story to London and "The Veterinary Journal" first took up the cudgels in reviewing his book**. The "Journal" lamented the scarcity of veterinary officers in India which was resulting in huge losses among horses through preventable disease, and continued:

Nothing can be more disgraceful than the neglect which allows such waste, unless it be the treatment to which the Indian Government subjects the officers of the Veterinary Department, nearly every one of whom is disgusted with the service in that part of our Empire.

Mr Meyrick has done his best to diminish the loss, suffering

*"History of the Royal Army Veterinary Corps" (Baillière, Tindall)
**Meyrick's book was entitled "A Veterinary Manual for the Use of Native Horse Owners in India."

and cruelty prevailing in the Hindustan, but so far as recognition is concerned for what would doubtless have obtained for him an honourable distinction, had he been serving in a foreign army, he is more likely to be ignored and snubbed and insulted through having his book submitted by the Government of India to some impertinent and ignorant doctor, or still-more ignorant and presumptious hanger-on.

Meyrick himself wrote a letter to the "Journal" (March 1882), revealing the appalling conditions under which army vets were working in India:

I have myself served nearly twelve years in India . . . The prospect is of unremitting slavery in an exhausting climate . . . very little leave . . . and the conditions ensure certain loss of health to nine out of ten men.

In May 1882 the "Journal" in a strong editorial, condemning the military authorities in India, said that they . . .

seem from all accounts to be bent on inflicting every kind of indignity on veterinary surgeons . . . The late campaign in Afghanistan has been the crowning indignity and has proved to be pretty well the last straw . . . Those veterinary surgeons who were at last called in to rescue the army from disaster were worked night and day until at last some died, others were invalided, and the remainder were all but overwhelmed with the effects of the climate, hardship and fatigue . . .

Meanwhile, unbeknown to him, Evans' theories on surra had by no means gone unnoticed. True, they aroused little interest in England, but elsewhere they were read with much attention in two of the most important research centres in Europe. In Berlin, the report (in "The Veterinary Journal") was studied by Robert Koch, founder of modern bacteriology. Koch, it is believed, made use of Evans' report when he investigated sleeping sickness in Africa in 1906/7. The report was also sent to Paris, where it was read by Louis Pasteur and commended by him to his students. Writing many years later in "The Veterinary Record", Dr R F Montgomerie said that it was largely through Pasteur and Koch's study of the report that Evans was eventually recognised as being the first to discover pathogenic trypanosome.

The man, however, who did most, in the immediately ensuing years, to ensure that Evans was credited with his achievement, was a keen young army veterinary surgeon named J H Steel. Steel was regarded as brilliant. He had launched an Indian veterinary journal and had also become principal of the Bombay Veterinary College. In 1885 he was sent to investigate a bad outbreak of surra among horses and mules in Burma. Evans was also asked to go to Burma, doubtless to give Steel the benefit of his experience and advice. It is ironical that in his report Steel hailed Dr Evans as the discoverer of the surra microbe, yet in his own investigations he identified the wrong parasite and diagnosed the wrong disease!

Evans described the incident many years later in a letter to his doctor daughter:

He (Steel) was very good at digesting and reproducing the work of others in new forms, and deficient in the ability for original observations and scientific deductions.

He observed so many inflamed stomachs of ponies post-mortem but failed completely in his deductions. I tried to persuade him that they were not related to surra . . . and I demanded a separate investigation. My opinion was that the inflammation was caused by some medicament. Steel did not press the investigation as he ought to have done.

He persisted in stating that the parasite I discovered was a spirillum that was well-known to the Germans. And he persisted in refusing to look at the parasite with my lens that magnified more and defined better than his own, a rather inferior quarter-inch, "because he was used to it."

Steel remained convinced that the surra parasite was a spirillum or spirochaete, which are bacteria associated with such diseases as relapsing fever or syphilis, and quite different from the flagellate protozoa which cause surra or sleeping sickness. He assumed that the horses were suffering from relapsing fever and proceeded to write his report on this assumption, entitling it, "An

Official Report on Relapsing Fever among Equines in British Burma". He gave Dr Evans full credit for discovering the microbe causing surra and named, or rather misnamed it *Spirochaeti evansi*. Writing in "The Veterinary Journal", he modestly said that his own achievement was merely to prove the pathological nature of the parasite and "to confirm Dr Evans' important discoveries." In fact, he did not so much confirm as confuse the truth.

Nevertheless, Griff welcomed this corroboration that the parasite he had discovered was indeed pathogenic and forgave Steel for the mistakes he had made. He paid handsome tribute in the official gazette to Steel's valuable work and recommended that he should be granted an honorarium.

Steel's mistake was soon corrected. The following year, the scientist Edgar Crookshank recognised the resemblance of Evans' microbe to a parasite of fish and named it *Haematomonas evansi*, later changing it to *Trichomonas evansi*. It was not, however, until ten years later (1896) that the Frenchman, Chauvrat, amended the name to *Trypanosoma evansi*.

The story was to have another ironic twist. Still a young man, Steel died in 1890 as a result of overnight exposure during research work in India. His friends, including Dr Evans, contributed towards a commemorative medal which was to become one of the principal awards bestowed by the Royal College of Veterinary Surgeons. Many years later, the Royal College decided that Dr Evans himself should be awarded the Steel Medal. And Griff, at the age of 83, accepted it in all humility, bearing no grudge against the young man to whom he had been mentor in the study of surra. But to his daughter, in a letter explaining the background of the award, he wrote:

I am amused and surprised by the honour of its being given to *ME*!

When they went to the Madras Presidency in March, 1881, the Evanses settled in Ootacamund, which liked to be called "the queen of the southern hill stations". Katie said she was enchanted by it and had never imagined such a place could exist in India. The cool climate, gentle rains and lovely green hills reminded her of Malvern: "and there is even a peak called Snowdon!"

Griff's duties took him far afield: to Bangalore and other military stations, and he had to spend much time in Madras City. But there was always Katie awaiting him in Ootacamund. They eventually took a house called Warley Lodge, although at first they lived at Sylk's Hotel. It was at Sylk's, on December 1, 1881, that Katie gave birth to a much-wished-for son whom Griff named Ywain Goronwy ap Griffith, leaving no doubt as to his ancestry.

The baby's ayah, according to Katie, was a gentle young woman, a convert to Roman Catholicism.

When I asked her why she prayed to the Virgin rather than directly to God, she replied: "If I break dish, I tell memsahib, memsahib she tell master."

When Ywain Goronwy ap Griffith was six months old, Katie was astonished to receive an anonymous note:

Dear Mrs Heavens, Be careful! Your ayah is going to poison you and your baby son. She is devil. Take care before it is too late.

With her husband absent in Bangalore, Katie was dismayed, yet could not imagine the doe-eyed ayah as a likely poisoner. Discreet inquiry showed that the note was penned by a neighbour's servant. Katie wrote to Griff:

It seems there is actually competition for the honour of looking after our son.

Griff replied:

Tell the servants that every single one of them will be put in gaol if anything happens to our baby or to you.

Right about this time the Evanses received a letter from James

Meyrick announcing that this resolute bachelor had, very reluctantly, at the age of 47, become married.* He explained that he had met his bride four years previously when on leave from India. They had gone to theatres together in London and he had invited her to bring her needlework while he worked on his book.

Meyrick's life was so closely linked with Griff's that his astonishingly frank letter justifies quotation:

I realised she thought I meant to propose to her. I was about to sail for India. I became engaged, but, soon after, wished I could break off the engagement. She is a delicate, sensitive creature just like Katie, and no larger, so I felt to say anything cruel would be like crushing a helpless little bird.

When I returned from India she seemed more passionately fond of me than ever, yet I had no actual love to give in return, except such as one feels for a sister. The thought of marrying one whom I did not love as a wife was terrible to me. Yet I could see no way of escape without being both dishonourable and inhuman. The only right course seemed to be to marry and so I determined to do so and leave the consequences to God.

The night before my marriage I was so furious at the thought of being forced by honour and humanity to marry against my will that I cursed myself and my wife, and hoped that I might tumble down dead or be smashed by a train. As I walked to the altar I felt a bitter hatred of the poor little thing though I knew the feeling would not last, and when she came she looked so frightened, and her hand trembled so much, that I could not help pitying her. I forced myself to go through with the marriage service with a calm voice, then went to a wedding breakfast at the Criterion.

What would any man of common sense have predicted of such a marriage as mine, but utter misery, at least for me? And yet I am now very happy. Day after day my love grew greater as I found out more and more of the wonderful goodness of my wife.

In a further letter, acknowledging congratulations, Meyrick

*His wife was Miss Elizabeth Henrietta Westbeare

176

explained that he had not told his friends of his engagement because he shrank from letting them know what an utter idiot he thought he had been:

> How little we know what is good for us! . . . I never felt such peace and happiness in my life, or such passionate love for anyone.

Meyrick lived to enjoy many years of happy marriage.*

In September 1882, a telegram brought news of the death of Griff's father at Borth-y-Gêst. He had hoped to return to Britain in time to see his father again, and it weighed on his conscience, as if he were to blame, that both his parents as well as his sister, Maria, had died while he was away from Wales. He kept the newspaper accounts of the funeral at Towyn for the rest of his life. The local paper said that all the shops were closed and every blind was drawn even by strangers "in tribute to a man universally admired for his sincerity and truthfulness, as well as his great powers in prose and song".

The following spring, 1883, Evans was promoted to the rank of lieutenant colonel.

That summer the Colonel's career might have come to a tragic end but for the resourcefulness of his wife. Their syce was driving them out of Ootacamund when the pony bolted and the trap overturned. Katie was flung clear but Griff was dragged across the road beneath the trap and pinned under a wheel where he lay in agony. Katie ran to him, shouting to the syce to hold the horse's head, and with almost superhuman strength that sometimes comes of crisis, she braced her small body to raise the side of the wheel so that her husband could release his trapped leg and then apply his own strength to release the rest of himself. His diary reads:

> I could not stand and was in great agony for hours. I certainly would have been killed if Katie had not the presence of mind and coolness to make such an effort to release me.

*Soon after his marriage he joined the expedition sent to deal with the rebellion in Egypt. Here he distinguished himself and was the first veterinary officer to be awarded the Companionship of the Bath in the Military Division – not to mention the Order of Osmanieh.

Was it that this incident engendered such a surge of affection between them that Katie became, very soon afterwards, pregnant again? Their fourth daughter was born on April 17, 1884.

Dreading that Griff's addiction for giving his daughters topographical names might lead to something like Ootacamunda, Katie said she wanted her baby to have simple Welsh names; she chose Mair Olwen. Their two born-in-India children were to be brought up speaking only Welsh at first. In fact, they spoke a strange language consisting of Welsh and numerous Hindustani words picked up from the servants.

During his years in Madras, Dr Evans persisted in his study of Eastern religions, and when he visited Burma with Steel he made voluminous notes on Buddhist customs there. At Ootacamund he joined a religious philosophical society, saying later: "This was the only secret society I was ever associated with. It helped me to useful knowledge and native friendships."

One day, Griff and Katie saw a couple riding into Ootacamund in a tonga coming from the plains. They were struck by the ethereal expression on the woman's face. Later they learned that she was Madame Blavatsky, founder of the Theosophical Society. She had come to Ootacamund with Colonel Olcott to study the Todas, the original inhabitants of the area. Dr and Mrs Evans invited the pair to luncheon at Warley Lodge.

It was a remarkable occasion.

Madame Blavatsky showed great interest in the numerous treasures Griff had collected during his years in India. First he showed her a copper image of Vishnu with consorts, tree and serpent, which had been to him by a Brahmin in a temple at Nazik; he explained that, most unfortunately, he had touched the image while admiring it and then was horrified to realise that in touching he had defiled it. The Brahmin, refusing his offer to pay for a purifying ceremony, said that the image had become no more than old metal and begged him to accept it as a gift. When Madame Blavatsky examined his brass chariot of the sun, a child's toy sold to him in Benares as being 4,000 years old, she exclaimed it was an imitation and he had been defrauded. What most impressed her was a piece of crystal, bought from a travelling pedlar in Simla. It was a prism, beautifully engraved with symbols. That was indeed a treasure, she said. The symbols had a most sacred and mystic significance, and she was astonished that any Hindu owner should have parted with it.

Russian-born Helene Pètrovna Blavatsky was then fifty-four.

She claimed to have been initiated into esoteric Buddhism and that she could perform supernatural feats with the aid of "Mahatmas", or spiritual teachers.

During luncheon, Katie and Griff were given evidence of her occult powers when they distinctly heard the sound of bells coming from somewhere between her shoulders and the ceiling. Griff later described them as like electric bells ringing in a vacuum; but apparently no comment was made at table. He questioned his guest closely about her "Mahatmas":

> The information she gave did not agree with what I already knew of India and the manners and customs of its inhabitants; and I told her so. Her answers became increasingly elusive, and she sought to change the subject.
> "They tell me," I said, "that you claim to be a hundred years old. Is that so?"
> "All I can tell you," Madame Blavatsky replied, "is that I was born in the last century."
> "By which calendar do you reckon, Madame? By the Christian, Mohammedan, Jewish, Hindu or Buddhist?"
> She laughed and said, "Doctor, you have guessed my riddle."

Griff later claimed that he forced her to admit that her celebrated phenomena were simply natural tricks. But he did not explain the trick of the bells. Katie's story was that she felt the conversation was becoming somewhat tense, and to create a diversion "accidentally" knocked some object off the table, and then changed the subject to the native customs of the Todas.

Dr Evans had almost completed his term of service in Madras. The attitude of the Indian Government towards him was now very different from what it had been in 1881. His opinions were repeatedly sought and several times he was asked to deal with problems beyond the Madras Presidency. Following his visit to Burma in 1885, he was urgently summoned to Bengal to deal with a veterinary crisis caused by the distribution of a dangerously inferior vaccine for anthrax.

Meanwhile, he and Katie were eagerly looking forward to being reunited with their three daughters in England. Griff had not seen the girls for eight years, and in some of his letters to them it seems that he did not realise they were no longer toddlers. He sent them childish jingles. To Towena, a practical young person who had long outgrown fairy stories, he wrote a tale of whimsy after the style of Charles Kingsley. He lacked Katie's facility for writing warm, human and humorous letters; sometimes, indeed, Victorian papa that he was, he wrote to his daughters as if he were taking a Sunday School class. For example:

My dear children, I am pleased with your little essays upon Happiness . . . Your essays lead me to believe that you do not clearly understand the difference between Happiness and Pleasure. I therefore enclose an explanation taken from Graham's Synonyms which I trust each of you will master for herself . . .
There is an active and a passive happiness. The active you will find is by far the better. It is derived by overcoming or conquering difficulties and evolving good out of apparent evil . . .

The letter continued on this theme for several more pages, and finished:

It is 11.30.pm. We are in an awfully grand thunderstorm which keeps me awake. The thunder shook the house and rattled things in this room. I am always happy in such a storm.
Your very loving father,
Griff.

Early in November, the C in C Madras, Lieutenant General Sir Frederick Roberts, sent Dr Evans a warm message congratulating him on the careful manner in which the Veterinary Department had carried out their duties, and adding that he would now be posted to Woolwich.

The Evanses embarked from Bombay on November 18, almost exactly five years since Katie had arrived in Calcutta.

CHAPTER SIXTEEN

The Queen Intervenes

London beckoned to Griff like a lode star as the ship left India behind. He was starved of research facilities, and impatient to prove to his colleagues that he had been right about the pathogenic significance of protozoa in the blood. Before that, he had to find a home for his family and settle into his new job at Woolwich.

Of all his years in the army, the next four under the Queen's Principal Veterinary Officer, George Fleming, were to prove the most unhappy. The only characteristics the two men had in common were first, intolerance and second, the conviction that their respective ideas were right. Fleming must have resented the outspoken way in which his not-very-tactful new staff officer contradicted some of his more dubious professional opinions, and even more the respect which his colleagues accorded to Evans' experienced views. Ultimately, there was open hostility between the two men regarding the treatment of the illness known as "roaring" in horses. Events were to prove Evans triumphantly right on this subject, for Fleming had attempted more than could be expected of his training and experience, and, as Sir Frederick Smith records, a cloud hung over his last years in the service, and he left in 1890 with a damaged reputation.

Evans had already suffered at his hands, for it was Fleming who had been editor of the "Veterinary Journal" at the time when Evans in India had complained of the way in which his report on surra had been cut and published in penny numbers. Fleming was a vain jealous man, anxious to be first in everything, and according to his biographer:*

". . . he was the victim of hero worship by the civil profession

*Sir Frederick Smith: "History of the Royal Army Veterinary Corps."

of this country to which he had rendered outstanding services; this did much to spoil a character that needed restraint rather than undue encouragement. His weaknesses were an incurable optimism, extra-ordinary impetuousity, a love of popularity and insatiable ambition."

He was also said to have suffered from the disadvantage of not having served in India, then regarded as the ultimate testing ground for army veterinary surgeons.

In the early spring of 1886, Evans called upon Professor Edgar Crookshank. This able young scientist was one of the few who had recognised the importance of Evans' discovery at Dera Ismail Khan. They had exchanged letters, and Evans had sent him specimens of surra-infected blood. Crookshank had worked with Pasteur and Koch, and had recently opened an up-to-date laboratory at King's College, London, for research into human and veterinary diseases.

He was aware of the strong difference of opinion between Evans and Timothy Lewis, and he had worked on, and given names to, the two strains of the microbe, one which Lewis had found in rats, and the other the parasite which Evans claimed was the cause of surra in horses.

Evans was nearing the end of his army service and felt he was at a turning-point. Still only fifty, he hoped he might have at least ten years to devote to medical research. He told Crookshank he wanted to use live monkeys, to demonstrate that the parasite Lewis had shown to be harmless in rats could be lethal in other animals. If it were indeed injurious to monkeys it might be established to be the cause not only of surra in horses and nagana in cattle but of sleeping-sickness in man. Crookshank was well-informed about the heavy toll of human and animal life which sleeping-sickness — later known as *trypanosomiasis* — was exacting in tropical countries, and he enthusiastically welcomed the older man's plans and said it was the ideal experiment for his new laboratory with its joint aim of serving mammals and humanity.

This was a period of strong anti-vivisectionist feeling. A recent law had made it obligatory to obtain a licence in order to carry out experiments with live animals. Evans thought this nonsense. Scientists, he argued, would not use animals for useless or frivolous experiments, and if they did, the new law would not stop them. He believed that the anti-vivisectionists actually perpetuated

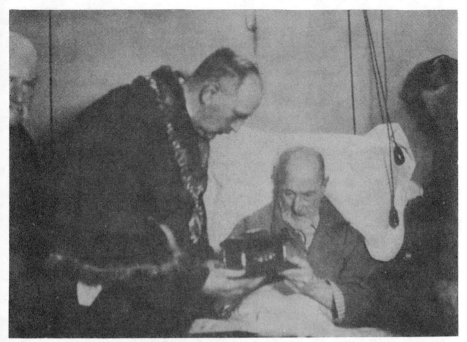

When they discovered the old doctor up the hill was a scientist of international repute they gave him the Freedom of the City.

"I am determined to walk again and take little grandson Griff on my *good* knee"

Brynhyfryd, Bangor. Noll Weber 9 Dec 1900

Dear Dr. Cunnis

In reference to your kind note dated 14 - received 29th ult - asking me to give you my photograph, I am glad you do not ask for more because at my age of 90 [...] with deficient sight to. I can write a little only, & slowly.

In your reference to my old friend Sir W. Osler offering me, and I send herewith a reprint from the Annals of Tropical Medicine and Parasitology with Photo - trusting you will not think I am too egoistic in so doing. The credit I take in reference to Trypanes - formed there for the Photographer.

Yours truly

Griffith Evans

—

I may of Philadelphia to the damp in 1880s - and have pleasant recollection of visiting the Patent Office, Museum, and Girard College to —

A specimen of Griffith Evans' handwriting in his nineties. Later, the then Duchess of York showed one of his letters to Princess Elizabeth, remarking: "Isn't it a simply marvellous piece of penmanship, for a man in his hundredth year?"

cruelty by refusing to recognise that it was better to sacrifice a tiny minority to save a multitude. However, he accepted Crookshank's advice and submitted his proposals to Joseph Lister, professor of Clinical Surgery at King's, and also to the Royal Colleges of Physicians and Surgeons. He was eventually granted a licence with the approval of all concerned.

In May, he was shocked to hear of the death from pneumonia of his rival, Timothy Lewis, at the early age of forty five years. He always claimed that, despite their differences, Lewis was his friend and he joined in the many tributes paid to that distinguished bacteriologist. Lewis' death was a blow because Evans was now denied the opportunity not so much of proving him wrong, but of establishing scientific truth in Lewis' mind and proving himself right! But he remained no less determined to press on with his experiments.

Then, a few weeks later, he appeared in the laboratory and announced gruffly that he had decided to abandon the whole project. Crookshank must have been very surprised, indeed astounded, but neither he nor anyone else could persuade him to say why. To everyone who knew Evans and the intensity of his zeal for this research, his sudden abandonment of it was a mystery, baffling in the extreme. It was not until long after his death that a letter came to light among the papers of Sir Frederick Smith at the Wellcome Library which revealed the secret behind this odd episode.

Smith, who was preparing his history of the Royal Army Veterinary Corps, in 1925 wrote to Evans asking him to explain his sudden decision in 1886. In his reply, the ninety-year-old Evans disclosed that it was Queen Victoria herself who had stopped his experiments. This, he said, must not be published in the "History;" he could repeat the facts only in the strictest confidence, as he had already done to Sir Harry Drinkwater, the medical historian.

The Queen had personally expressed the desire that he should not continue with his experiments on live monkeys and had asked that the licence granted to him should be withdrawn. Her wishes were conveyed to him in a private interview with an un-named official, who asked that Evans should not divulge from whom the request had come. Griff told Sir Frederick Smith that throughout his life he had

". . . insisted on not publishing the 'why-not' while I lived because it involved the direct interference of the Queen, which was given and explained to me privately . . . "

Loyal as he was to the Queen, whose "trusty and well-beloved Gentleman" he was, her intervention came as the bitterest of blows. Without tests on living animals he could make no further useful contribution towards proving the pathogenic nature of protozoa. He continued to take an interest in the bacteriological work going on at Crookshank's laboratory but the Queen's veto had, in effect, ended his career as a research scientist.

Who told the Queen about Evans' project? What induced her to take this unusual action against one of her senior officers?

Her Majesty detested vivisection. But she would not have concerned herself with the granting of individual licences. Apart from Crookshank, and the licensing authorities, who had already sanctioned the experiments, very few people knew of Evans' plans. The objection must have been raised after the licence was issued. For this reason, the finger of suspicion points at Evans' chief, the Queen's Principal Veterinary Officer, George Fleming, who would have access to Her Majesty's advisers and enough authority to upset Evans' arrangements.

Rightly or wrongly, Evans had not thought it necessary to tell his chief about his project until the licence had been granted, as his research was to be carried out only in his leisure time. This lack of communication was hardly surprising because as mentioned earlier, the two men had been in violent disagreement almost from the moment when Evans walked into Fleming's office and reported for duty as one of his senior staff officers.

Apart from his jealousy, there are other reasons why George Fleming may have thought it right to put a stop to the private researches of his Inspecting Veterinary Surgeon. In his role as editor of "The Veterinary Journal", he would have been well aware of the churlish manner in which the Government of India had treated Evans' report on surra. He would also know that Griff had the reputation of being something of a trouble-maker with a bee in his bonnet about the cause of surra, and that this had led to his posting to Madras. It is likely that Fleming feared he would continue his trouble-making in England, and that the research he planned was merely a means of pursuing a personal vendetta against Timothy Lewis. Now that Lewis had died, Fleming may well have imagined that it was his duty to prevent Lewis' distinguished reputation from being damaged by this truculent and argumentative Welshman, perhaps to the detriment of the army veterinary service.

Evans, in fact, had no intention of carrying out a vendetta against Lewis. But certainly a less uncompromising man would have handled Fleming with more tact. As it was, Griff undoubtedly felt bitter towards his chief for the rest of his life, although he was reluctant to go into detail over their quarrel.

Fleming was not friendly towards me because I would not say "ditto" to all he said when I was certain he was wrong and acting against the interests of the service.

Naturally, the two officers had to conceal their animosity on many public occasions, especially during the summer of Queen Victoria's Golden Jubilee, when they sat together at the great service in Westminster Abbey. The efforts of Fleming's predecessor, Collins, had resulted in a veterinary surgeon no longer being *persona non grata* at royal levees, and on St David's Day, 1887, George Fleming and Griffith Evans represented the veterinary service at the Jubilee Levee in St James' Palace.

Fleming had to present Evans to the Prince of Wales, and standing next to the Prince, resplendent in his uniform of Field Marshal, stood the Duke of Cambridge, still commander-in-chief of the British Army. He chatted to Evans briefly about his service in India. That evening, with one of his wry flashes of humour, Griff told Katie that he had thought it inadvisable to reveal himself to the Duke as the young subaltern who had refused to salute him in Kensington a quarter of a century before!

Many honours were distributed on the occasion of the Queen's Jubilee. Dr George Fleming received the Companionship of the Bath. No honour, military or civil, was conferred on Dr Griffith Evans.

During this unhappy spell, Griff, who had settled his family in Victorian comfort at 208 Burrage Road, Plumstead, found great solace and sympathy in his wife. Katie knew that the frustration in his professional life was not the only disappointment he had suffered on his return to England.

The reunion with his three elder children had proved less joyful than he had imagined it during his Indian solitude.

From the moment he saw them waiting on the railway platform, he realised he did not know them, and worse, that they did not know him. He had parted in 1877 from three small girls; Wynona, six; Erie, four; and Towena still a toddler. He was now shyly greeted by three half-fledged young women with whom he felt ill at ease. Only Wynona had any clear memory of him as a playful dada who used to give them piggy-backs; and his ponderous letters had given little stimulation to the children's imagination of him. Now they saw him as an old man, prematurely aged by the heat of India, brusque, gaunt and tetchily impatient. And they sensed that he was somehow disappointed in them.

He was, indeed, disappointed that they had picked up so little of his native language during their holidays in Wales. He was even more disappointed, and angry, to find that the strict chapel to which they had been escorted each Sunday from their boarding-school had filled their heads with the most Calvinistic of hell-fire Methodism. His anger was unreasonable since their religious instruction was doubtless little more narrow and orthodox than that given in most girls' private schools of the period, in fact hardly more so than what they would have encountered amongst their Welsh relations on their holidays in Borthy-Gêst.

Griff, the freethinker, could not play on muted strings, and, with the overbearing manner developed during his years of authority in India, he commanded his daughters to jettison all they had learned about a literal hell-fire, heaven and predestination. They had been wickedly indoctrinated, and must discredit much of the Old Testament. They must learn, and live by, the Sermon on the Mount.

Yet, at their new day-school and their Congregational Sunday School the poor girls were still instructed according to those narrow Victorian precepts which their father condemned. They must have been very confused indeed. However, Wynona and Towena were seemingly not particularly worried, having a girlish unconcern for religious dogma; but the intense, earnest and devout Erie was shocked. She recoiled from a father who had tried to destroy her faith.

Nor was religion the only stumbling block to harmonious family life. The girls' parents had returned from India with two smaller children, Goronwy, aged four, who spoke only Welsh and Hindustani, no English at all, and the baby Mair, eighteen months old. Inevitably, the three older girls regarded these newcomers at

186

first as strangers, and were even jealous that they had something of which for five years they had been deprived – their mother's loving presence. Their father aggravated the emotional chasm by insisting that Welsh should continue to be the first language of the two youngest children. Two monoglot Welsh maid-servants were duly installed at 208 Burrage Road.

Griff said he wanted his children to be "united like a bundle of sticks," and Katie agreed that they must devise ways of making them so. She thought the elder girls should be encouraged to take the little ones under their wings. Erie was given the baby Mair as her special charge, to care for and to sleep with at night. Towena was to have little Goronwy as her room-mate for a year or two. Wynona, as the eldest, was given a room to herself and told she must keep an eye on all four younger ones. This seemed a sensible plan, but in practice it proved disastrous, merely converting the horizontal split into a vertical one. Erie and Mair formed a lifelong devotion; Towena, the rebel, championed her little brother and he became over-dependent upon her; and the independent Wynona irritated all the others by her constant bossiness, fault-finding and tale-bearing. The Evans children remained thus divided.

Cheated of a scientific career, Griff resolved to live in Wales on his retirement from the army. He suggested to Katie that they should go on a holiday tour to decide on a retirement location, but, with her usual wisdom, she stood back. It was Erie, she said, who should be his companion for this trip. She saw it as an ideal opportunity for him to win back his estranged daughter. Her intuition was right. During their week walking and climbing in Snowdonia, Griff and Erie established a bond which was to endure until death separated them. The pretty fifteen-year-old was intelligent and serious-minded beyond her years. She shared her father's love of mountains and his deep interest in medicine and religion. She abandoned her God of Calvinistic Methodism and worshipped her father instead, always afterwards speaking of "Father" with an audible capital F, reverencing his opinions and judgment while he lived, giving up her medical career to serve him in his old age; and, when he died, treasuring and preserving his writings like Holy Writ.

In later years, Griff came to understand his initial error in his handling of the adolescent Erie, and wrote to her:

When I returned from India I soon discovered the dangerous net in which you and your sisters were entangled, and I did my best in much anxiety to help you work your own way into the freedom of Jesus . . .

Whether I applied the wrench in the best way for you is, I admit now, open to doubt. I am sincerely sorry for any unnecessary pain and spiritual trouble my want of judgment may have caused you. I did not have your early experience of – may I say? – orphanhood. It was orphanhood to a great degree. And you dear little girls were longing so much for the return of your lost parents, whom you idealised and idolised. But when they did return, you found them so different from your ideals!

It was a sore trial, and life is so short to make amends.

Dy Dad anwyl . . .

After the little holiday, Griff's diary reflects a much cosier family association.

Woolwich. *August 7 1889:*

My birthday. With my family at the Crystal Palace, Sydenham. We drove there and back in my wagonette.

In a month's time he left for Curragh Camp, near Dublin. Inspecting Veterinary Surgeons in their last year of service were usually given the post of IVS Ireland, but, as Griff told his children, this would be only a "separation within reach".

Curragh. *September 6, 1889:*

Took over the duties of IVS Ireland from my old friend Meyrick, who retires from the Army today.

Griff wrote from the Curragh to Katie that he was appalled by the degeneration in Ireland's relations with England since they were at Curragh Camp when the children were small. He believed the Irish were being unfairly treated and that their demands would increase in ratio to Westminster's refusal to meet them. He was convinced that Ireland must be given home rule.

That autumn, he spent his first few days of leave in house-hunting with Katie in Bangor, North Wales, which they had decided was preferable to his beloved Towyn as a place of retirement because of its good educational facilities, including a new University College.

He had to pay £1,200 for the house they chose, Brynkynallt, and another £400 for alterations – new grates in all the rooms, a porch and an indoor lavatory. Back in Curragh he made himself ill with worry at having paid such a high price, and Katie had to hurry to Dublin to nurse him for bronchitis.

December 6 1889
    Dear Katie arrived without delay. So glad to see her. It made me feel much better.

A month later, he was urgently summoned home to Plumstead where Mair, the five-year-old, was dangerously ill with meningitis.

The family doctor had given up hope. Griff took over from him, saying he thought he could save his daughter. He had taken charge of Goronwy in India when, at the age of three, the child had nearly died of a severe fever with convulsions. Griff now treated Mair for perforated tympanum, and stayed by her bed day and night.

Katie had complete faith in his skill. He had saved Goronwy, now he would save Mair. And, indeed, for the third time in his life, Griff's treatment and intensive care brought back a child from the gates of death when other doctors said they could not.

At the end of July, 1890, Griff made the journey from Ireland to London for the last time, and escorted his family to North Wales. Now a full Colonel, he retired from the army on his fifty-fifth birthday.

CHAPTER SEVENTEEN

A Liberal in the Land of Lloyd George

July 23 1890
>   Furniture arrived from Woolwich
August 7 1890
>   Retired. Settling down at Brynkynallt.

Griffith Evans was settling down indeed. At Brynkynallt he was to spend the last forty-five of his hundred years. He rarely slept under any other roof.

To a Bangor friend he wrote:

> I have been knocking about the world with all sorts and conditions of men since I left home as a lad of eighteen. So I am more out of touch with my native country than I would wish to be.

Tradesmen soon began to recognise the austere colonel who had come to live in the house on the hill. But when they greeted him with a "Good morning, Colonel Evans!" he would reply brusquely: "Plain Dr Evans, please! Retired from the army now."

At fifty-five he still possessed enormous energy, both physical and mental, and during the next two decades threw himself into a vast range of activity. The pleasant little city of Bangor was proud of its new University College and there the doctor quickly made his presence felt. He agreed to lecture on veterinary hygiene for one year, and made use of college facilities to undertake some useful if unspectacular research. He was persuaded to continue lecturing for twenty years, finally retiring in 1910, when he was almost seventy-five. During those years he was concerned with the growth of the college and personally influenced the purchase of the Bishop's palace and park to make way for a new arts building.

He became embroiled in controversies on local politics, free trade, home rule for Ireland, religion, suffragettes, total abstinence, or whatever was in season. He wrote innumerable letters to the Press. Bangor soon came to regard him as an eccentric. The hill on which he lived was known as Lonpopty, literally "the way of the oven", and it was as if the oven had suddenly become a volcano, ever in danger of eruption.

He read prodigiously, especially science, history and political and moral philosophy. He browsed through the nineteenth century novelists. He had the infuriating habit of pencilling comments in the margins of his books. In his well-used copy of "Anna Karenina" – "the world's greatest novel" – he seems to be conducting a personal dialogue with Tolstoy – "the world's greatest novelist". When Levin soliloquises on reason and faith, Griff observes in the margin: "Faith begins where true knowledge ends; it leads to evil as often as good."

He studied and annotated all the scientific periodicals. As the veterinarian R F Montgomerie was later to remark, there was no major new scientific development that escaped his notice.

Katie, now a matron of forty-seven, loved her new home, and was thankful her nomadic life was over. She made Brynkynallt into a warm, welcoming home, smelling of spices, apples and polished oak. Her gossipy tea-parties became a local legend. Sometimes the doctor would look in to greet the ladies, but one suspects they felt a sense of relief when he withdrew to his study. On summer days, Katie served tea in the garden, and once she was dismayed to observe her guests holding handkerchiefs to their noses. The source of the unpleasant smell was the orchard, where the doctor had hung rows of bottles of milk, uncorked, on the apple trees. After removing them he explained that he was studying micro-organisms in putrid milk, and had found much dirt in the milk from the local farms and dairies, mostly from cow-dung. He hastened to reassure the alarmed ladies that, by Hindus in India, cow-dung was regarded as a purifier.

Griff and Katie loved to climb the mountains. They had not been a month in Bangor before they took the family up Snowdon – a single file crocodile of father, mother, four daughters, one son and two dogs; and for years after their children had left home they would set off on their own. A friend fishing in Crafnant Lake once spied them coming over the hill from Capel Curig.

I was startled to see high up on the mountain skyline, appearing in full sail, a lady in a bonnet, cape and billowing black skirt. I knew it could only be Mrs Evans, Brynkynallt, out on one of her fell walks with the doctor.

Griff's politics were moderately liberal; he disliked both Marxism and Imperialism. He summed up his views to Erie:

> Liberalism involves liberty for each individual to better himself as much as he can so long as he does not prevent others doing so. Socialism means, not freedom, but strict government by bureaucracy. Imperialism may be compared to cancer in the human body . . . Ancient and modern imperialism has always destroyed itself by its own growth.

He admired the young David Lloyd George who several times stayed at Brynkynallt. During the Boer War, he accompanied him to a meeting in a Bangor chapel, and sat on the platform with Katie as the future Prime Minister tried to make a pro-Boer speech. An angry audience pelted Lloyd George with rotten eggs and tomatoes, and when Katie's bonnet was knocked askew, Griff took her and his guest out of the building by a back door to escape the hostile crowd in the High Street. Accompanied by a policeman, they scrambled up a dark wood and into Brynkynallt garden by a side gate. Next morning, Mair Evans, then in her late teens, asked Ll G. for his autograph, and he wrote in her book: "Let us march always with our faces towards the dawn – Victor Hugo."

The side gate through which Lloyd George found refuge was constructed by Dr Evans in defiance of Lord Penrhyn, the local slate magnate, with whom he was in dispute over a right of way on Bangor "mountain". Every day, the doctor would go through the gate and up the path, removing any barricades erected to keep the citizens out.

For most of his life, he had insisted that he was an agnostic, but once retired to Bangor he regularly attended Sunday morning service at Pendref Congregational Chapel. Because of his deafness he always sat in the front pew, hand cupping ear, his current Welsh terrier peeping between his boots. Unmoved by any emotional *hwyl*, he fixed his gaze upon the preacher and after the service would sometimes pursue him into the vestry and challenge him on points in his sermon. Once at a missionary meeting, he stood up and uttered what at that time was heresy: he accused missionaries of "creating curry and rice Christians by bribing good Hindus with gifts of food to renounce their excellent faith."

Another of his heresies was the belief that girls who had "love children" should not be penalised. He shocked the chapel by declaring that such girls were not wicked, but simply too kind to men.

He was a member of the Rationalist Press Association but despite his known rationalist views his offer to take a class of students at the Pendref Chapel Sunday School was accepted, and later he even became superintendent of the Sunday School . . . It is interesting to speculate whether there was any other member of the Association who was also a Congregational school teacher.

It was the custom for the superintendent to hear the children recite their "adnod," a verse from the Bible, in front of the assembly. Griff used to tell of a little boy who was "too terrified to speak a single word and would not stop weeping. I asked him just to whisper one verse to me. The child sobbed out, 'Jesus wept'. I was crushed and could not think of anything to say."

Among his early friends at the University College was Professor Henry Jones*, a humanitarian with a great sense of humour, who was to become one of the leading philosophers of his day. They spent many hours in verbal conflict, which Jones apparently enjoyed, but it seems they could agree on nothing except that Welsh terriers were the best dogs to have.

When in 1905, Professor Jones was writing a work on the current religious revival in Wales, he sent a request to Evans from Glasgow, asking him to comment. The reply was characteristic:

> I am an agnostic in line with Herbert Spencer and Huxley . . . Last summer I was publicly labelled a materialist . . . I do not object to that label if it means only my disagreement with metaphysical idealism. I am not in sympathy with extreme emotional demonstrations of a religious revival . . .
> A. I believe it is good for people to be religious.
> B. No religion can be good, effectively, unless it is emotional. A profession of religion is either sincere, with some degree of enthusiasm, or else it is a sham. Of all shams, a sham religion is the worst.
> C. Every man's religion ought to be his own.
> D. Full freedom should be allowed everyone to express his religion in his own way so long as he does not interfere with the freedom of others.

* Later Sir Henry Jones C.H., Professor of Moral Philosophy at Glasgow University.

193

Evans always supported the feminist movement. He admired Mrs Pankhurst's campaign for women's suffrage and consistently advocated the extension of educational opportunities for women. When he arrived in Bangor, he at once registered his elder daughters as students at the University College, the two younger girls following in due course. But none of the four stayed to take a degree. The only intellectual among them, his second daughter Erie, left in order to study medicine in London. In the late eighteen-nineties she qualified and put up her plate in Cardiff, where she practised for many years. She was an attractive girl but never married. She had her father's keen intellect and a deep interest in science and religion. They corresponded regularly, and she spent most of her holidays in Brynkynallt. She treasured his letters and on his death devotedly ensured that his diaries and other papers were preserved in the National Library of Wales. They rarely discussed medical matters by letter, but Erie kept a few of his comments:

October 1916 Your case of the woman who had perforated gastric ulcer from worry about her two brothers – feeling that they are guilty of murder in fighting the Germans – is interesting, showing the effect of wrong religious dogmas upon some abnormal states of mind. If a man came to me with a sword or pistol threatening to maim or kill me, I would not hesitate to kill him first, if I could anyhow.

January 1928 (He was then 92) Surgeons are mistaken in concentrating attention on cancer cells. The cause of an overgrowth in cancer cells is lack of vitality in the neighbouring cells.

The eldest daughter, Wynona, had inherited the dominating character of her great-grandmother Mary Evans (of the ill-fated golden dowry), though she had never shown much power of concentration. She was able to escape from academic study when her mother's uncle, a well-to-do Montgomeryshire farmer named Owen Jones, invited her to come and keep house for him with a view to being his heiress. He had recently scandalised the district by burying his wife in his garden instead of in the churchyard. Wynona settled happily as mistress of Gelli Farm and, when at the age of forty she married a rich Sheffield manufacturer, she stipulated that they should make their home with Uncle Owen until he died.

The third daughter, Towena, was passionate, impulsive and emotionally unstable, like Griff's mother, the other Mary Evans. Despite the strict segregation of the sexes at College, she managed to meet and fall in love with a senior student, and when he proposed to her she escaped from book-learning as her father sent her to a domestic science college "to learn to be a poor man's wife". Her husband had the offer of a teaching post in Pwllheli, and teachers were not well-paid. Griff accepted with stoicism the news that his future son-in-law was the son of a Yorkshire brewer.

Emotionally, Griff was most drawn to his youngest daughter Mair. She was a shy girl who had inherited the charm, sympathy and humour of her mother. Her University career ended when she was badly injured in the gymnasium. As part of her convalescence her father took her with him to a scientific conference in Stockholm, and there she conceived the idea of becoming a Swedish masseuse. Griff encouraged her to stay two years in Stockholm to qualify, and later she came home to practice in North Wales. In 1913, she married Harry Jones, the eldest son of her father's old friend, Professor Henry Jones. Harry was in the Indian Civil Service and Mair was to go out to Burma with him. Her father said that as she would have servants she would not need to learn domestic science, and instead he sent her to London with a purse of sovereigns to buy herself a trousseau at Liberty's.

Griff's only son Goronwy was a dissappointment. He lacked intellectual brilliance, but this was not the reason. He was good with his hands, and an excellent draughtsman, and after training as a naval architect he finished up as a practising architect in Towyn. Sadly, he suffered from the weakness of his Evans ancestors – delusions of grandeur. He was a heraldic snob and built a baronial fireplace in his small bungalow, hanging above it the crest of a sixth century Welsh king from whom he claimed descent. He was obsessed with his pedigree, and when his father laughed at him, he dropped his surname to become known as Goronwy ap Gruffydd. His wife died childless and he used to refer to himself as "the last of the line" although his father had nine grandchildren. He arranged to be buried in the grave of his ancestor, Evan ap Jenkin.

Throughout his hundred years, Griff rarely went to a theatre. Perhaps it was because of his difficulty in hearing, perhaps because of his intense realism, but the make-believe of the stage had no appeal for him. However, before they sailed to Burma, Mair and her husband, Harry Jones, invited her parents to see a performance of "Charley's Aunt". The outing was not a success. As he sat with his hand to his ear, the doctor became more and more exasperated. At last, surrounded by people falling about with laughter, he roared: "I cannot see anything funny in this play at all!"

In 1921, he fought a fierce postal battle with the dramatist John Drinkwater, who in his play "Abraham Lincoln", portrayed General Ulysses Grant as a drunkard with slurred speech, forever swallowing whisky. Griff, who was then eighty-six, wrote to the playwright claiming that he had been a guest of the American general for a week during the Civil War, and had personal knowledge that Grant was a teetotaller, although he had been a heavy drinker before his fiancée had asked him to abstain. He submitted that it was wrong to distort history for dramatic effect.

I trust you will take kindly to this criticism by an old man who wishes you well, as he does the memory of those who were very kind to him long, long ago.

Drinkwater wrote a friendly reply, saying that he had asked the actor playing Grant to modify his performance. He refused, however, to alter the text. Griff continued his letters of protest, and to pacify him Drinkwater altered the stage instruction "Speech thick". The old doctor continued to carry on his offensive, claiming that Drinkwater's "cruel injustice travestied history, and caused pain to the General's friends", and demanding that the text be corrected. Drinkwater, who probably doubted whether any more of the General's friends still survived, sent a curt final reply:

To G Evans Esq. Thank you for your letter. There is in the text nothing which indicates that Grant did more than take a glass of whisky at reasonable intervals, and I am afraid that I do not look upon that as an evil habit.

Alcohol was a subject on which Griffith Evans seemed at times to overstep the bounds of rationality. He apparently regarded it as worse for Grant to be labelled as a drunkard than to be responsible for the ruthless sacrifice of American lives in a campaign of savage attrition. To Griff, a drunken man was a degraded man, and certainly during much of his life in Wales, drink was a major evil, and children did indeed go hungry because workers were spending so much of their pay on alcohol. Katie used to say that she was thankful her husband's deafness prevented him from hearing the drunks singing as they staggered home on Saturday nights up Lonpopty. He vigorously and successfully crusaded for the conversion of a number of North Wales public houses into temperance hotels.

It was not until his eighty-first year, in the middle of the Great War, that he was "discovered" by the outside world. It happened as a result of a meeting of the North Wales Branch of the British Medical Association in support of a plan to give Wales its own national school of medicine. The chief speaker was his old friend, Sir William Osler, Regius Professor of Medicine at Oxford.

Osler pointed to the octagenarian sitting in the body of the hall and told the meeting about Evans' achievements in India. To several scientists it came as a revelation that Griffith Evans was still alive. From that moment tributes were showered upon him. In 1917, the Liverpool School of Tropical Medicine honoured him with the Mary Kingsley Medal for "distinguished service in the cause of tropical medicine by original research". Next came the Royal College of Veterinary Surgeons with the award of their coveted John Henry Steel Memorial Medal. Soon afterwards, the University of Wales gave him an honorary Doctor of Science degree, "for his pioneer research in parasitology".

Earlier, the Army had awarded him a distinguished service pension, and the local paper had reprinted a tribute to him from the Indian Journal of Veterinary Science, adding:

Dr Evans is well-known in Bangor as a stalwart Free Churchman and Liberal, always ready to express his opinions without fear or favour, and never truckling to public opinion . . . But many in Bangor may not be aware that in the outside world Dr Evans is known as a scientist.

The Indian journal had referred to him throughout its tribute in the *past* tense, as if he were already dead. Griff passed the paper to his wife, chuckling. He said, "Os mynni glod, bid farw, Katie fach!"*

In 1931, he was presented with the Freedom of the City of Bangor. But this honour, the one dearest to his heart, he could not share with his wife. It came eight years too late. Katie had died in 1923.

* If you want glory, you must die, Katie dear!"

CHAPTER EIGHTEEN

The Long Sunset

One evening, a few days before his eighty-eighth birthday, Griff wrote to Erie: "Sometimes I am overpowered, failing to find her."

Earlier he had returned from his walk. He rang the bell to let the maids in the kitchen know he was back for supper. The dogs ran into the dining room, and through the open door he could see the table set for one. Katie's wing chair, from which she had always risen to greet him, cried out its emptiness.

He went upstairs, where his bed was made for one; Katie's pillow had been taken away. He could hardly believe it was little more than a week since they had gone up together and she said, "I've had such a happy day." Then, in the early hours, he felt her hand clutch his. She died in his arms.

In the lonely months that followed, he doggedly continued his routine, rising at 6.30, tapping his barometer, taking out his dogs, attending his committees. He tried to keep going the little winter garden Katie had grown in the glass porch, but her plants died.

On the fifty-fifth anniversary of his betrothal he wrote to Erie – the only one to whom he confided his despair – that he wished he could be in Montgomeryshire "to wander alone by the banks of the River Banwy where we two walked together that day." Then he quoted from Coleridge:

A grief without a pang, void, dark and drear,
A stifled, drowsy, unimpassioned grief
Which finds no natural outlet, no relief
In word or sigh or tear.

Erie came home as often as her practice would permit. They would hire a horse-drawn cab and drive to Lake Ogwen, and from there walk up to their favourite mountain tarns. These were the scenes which for thirty years he had shared with Katie.

When, in February 1925, James Meyrick died at 91, Griff received a letter from Dr Fred Bullock:

"The honour of being the father of the veterinary profession now falls upon you who were his junior as a graduate by only a week."

The "honour" was scant consolation for the loss of his oldest friend. Reporters who came to interview him found him unresponsive. He wrote a testy letter to Erie:

I wish they would leave me alone. I do not like being flattered in public. I rather gratify myself, chuckling, in thinking of some good I may have done the public not aware of me.

He reached the bottom of his well of desolation when he broke his left leg the following month. He was found lying on Bangor "mountain", his dogs whimpering beside him. He was carried home, and as he lay in bed, the realisation that he would never stride again over the hills and that he must part with his dogs, was harder to bear than the physical pain.

He summoned the vet. "My dogs, Tango and Dell. I shall be no further use to them. I want you to put them down."

When the dogs had been taken away, he lay very still. Erie came to his bedside. She said: "Mair's baby has arrived. It's a boy and they are naming him Griffith after you."

Griff said nothing for a moment. Then, looking proud and pleased, he told her that he was determined to walk again and "take little Griffith on my *good* knee."

Erie now faced the problem of finding somebody to care for her father in her absence. It was in this dilemma that she discovered Ellen. The two young servants, who had no wish to be nursemaids to a crippled old man, had handed in their notice. Yet, at that time in North Wales, there were still plenty of girls willing to go into domestic service, even to care for a bedridden man of ninety. And in Ellen, although she was so young, Erie

200

detected qualities which the others lacked. She saw a smiling, auburn-haired girl of spirit, thin and underfed, but wiry. Her brown eyes were intelligent and kind; her hands showed that she was no stranger to hard work. Her mother was a widow and she was one of the elder of eight children. Times were hard. She needed the job.

As Erie took her upstairs to see the Doctor, the girl said she had "never even spoken to a gentleman as old as ninety."

Ellen had a remarkable memory, and, in her sixties, she could still recall almost every word of her first talk with old Dr Evans. She was not upset by the loudness of his voice because Erie had told her he used to be a soldier, and warned her to speak up too, because he was hard of hearing. So when he shouted in Welsh, "How old are you Ellen?" she shouted back in the same language with no shyness "Twenty!"

"Where do you live?"

"Gerlan".

"I know it well. Under the mountain Yr Elen. I have often scrambled down it after crossing the 'saddle'. Were the mountains clear today? I can't climb any more now, Ellen. My leg is broken."

He paused and added:

"But I intend to walk again, you know."

"And I will help you," Ellen replied.

Erie's instinct was right. Ellen, though quite untrained, proved to be a born nurse. She tackled the physical needs of a bedridden old man sensibly and without qualm. She was as pleased as he was when at last he took his first step in the bedroom, and Griff was delighted when she said:

"We will try for one extra step every day until you get to the landing!"

"That is right, Ellen! 'Softlee, softlee catchee monkey!' "

Ellen understood.

"Slowly does it!" she said.

Few things surprised her; but one day when he announced that the barber would be visiting him to cut his hair, she stared at his bald pate in astonishment. She could see only a stubbly growth round the base of his skull. She soon realised, however, that the barber's three-weekly visit was an important event, necessary for the Doctor's self-respect. He insisted on wearing his overcoat to sit at the dressing table for his haircut. He thought it unmanly to appear in a dressing gown before the barber. Every day he would brush his few hairs vigorously with a hard-bristle brush so that there would be something for the barber to trim.

"Movement and growth is life, Ellen; stagnation is death. However old you are, you must always bestir yourself."

He made such progress with his walking that soon he was able, with great care, to go downstairs and to do without the night-nurse Erie had engaged for him.

Early one morning, the house was burgled. But Griff had risen before Ellen was up, and the intruder heard a great clearing of a masculine throat and the sound of clumping feet coming down the stairs. He fled, taking with him nothing more than Griff's overcoat, which the police retrieved in time for the barber's next visit.

Every week, Ellen went home to see her mother and her "young man", Jack Williams, and when she came back she would tell Griff the village gossip. Once in 1926, she said that Jack was pleased because "LI G" had sided with the Labour Party over the General Strike.

"I used to know Lloyd George," Griff told her. "He often came to this house."

As Griff gradually needed less nursing, she took up the duties of a secretary, running up and down stairs fetching files and books from his study. She marvelled at the exactitude with which he told her where to find each book on each shelf. She went to the bank and the post office for him, and even mastered her terror of the telephone to pass on his messages to the many people in the University and town with whom he kept in touch. In the spring of 1927, she shared his triumph when he reached the seat outside on the patio to enjoy the sunshine, and at last kept his promise to take his grandson, Griffith, on his knee.

Then fate struck another blow. One morning he could not hear what Ellen said to him. He ordered "fortiphones" and asked her to count aloud into them while he watched her lips. But when she reached six – the Welsh *chwech* – which should have been violently audible – he cast the instrument aside.

"Oh Ellen! Ellen! I am stone deaf now! Totally cut off!"

Ellen swiftly adapted to communicating with him by writing on his bedside pad. And now that the world around him had become silent, his face took on a new repose because he no longer had to suffer the strain of listening. Gone was his lifelong gesture of cupping his ear with his hand.

In the autumn of 1929 came further distaster. As he moved about in his bedroom during the night, he fell and fractured his right femur. He shouted for help until he was hoarse, but Ellen was a heavy sleeper and did not hear him. At last he hauled himself up the bedpost and lay across the bed, where Ellen found him next morning exhausted and voiceless.

The doctor told him he would never leave his bed again. Ellen blamed herself for having slept so soundly, but Griff reassured her.

"Don't you worry, I shall walk again," he said.

She wrote on his pad: "Of course you will. We've done it once and we'll do it again."

He was now in his ninety-fifth year. He never again walked down the stairs, but with Ellen's aid he did eventually succeed in shuffling from one to another of the bedrooms on the first floor, deserted rooms where his daughters had once slept. He made this his daily exercise.

One dreary day, when the rain beat steadily against the windows, he rested on the edge of one of the shrouded beds and covered his face with his hands.

"Ellen, I am so lonely. My dear, dear wife is not here."

He was now obliged to take his meals in bed. Nothing upset him more than to drop a crumb on the sheet or splash his dressing-jacket. Once, when he was particularly apologetic, Ellen wrote: "Please don't be sorry. You are *always* like a soldier."

The diet which took him into his 101st year contained plenty of butter. In preparing his trays Ellen had to adhere strictly to what he prescribed himself. For breakfast at 7:30 he had bread and milk with two ounces of butter and syrup one morning, treacle the next. For lunch he had finely-minced meat with a raw egg and two more ounces of butter beaten in, with a spoonful of yeast-extract stirred in at the end (on alternate days he had boiled onions instead.) Precisely half an hour after luncheon, he drank China tea without milk or sugar. At 6.30 pm he had milk and wheat-germ food, and at nine o'clock, when Ellen handed over to the night-nurse, she brought a tray, with apple juice for his 2 am drink, orange juice to be taken at 6 am, and a night-light to burn beside his bedside clock.

As he slowly recovered from the shock of his fractured thigh, Griff's intellectual life took on a new lease. He began a fresh study of psychology and made copious notes, often showing shrewd and prophetic judgment. For instance:

Animals have a great capacity for acclimatising themselves

to changing circumstances. But a whole species can perish if the change is too sudden or too severe. It is probable that man's scientific development is outpacing his psychological evolution, and I doubt if human psychology can adapt itself with sufficient speed to survive the rapidly-changing conditions of this century. This may mean that in the next few decades there will be a serious increase in the incidence of mental diseases.

One day he looked up to see Ellen standing beside him twisting the pad in her hands. She had not touched him to announce her presence as she usually did.

"What is it, Ellen?"

She sat down and slowly wrote:

"Jack has asked me to marry him."

For several moments Griff did not speak. He covered one hand with the other. They were trembling. His voice shook, too, when he asked:

"What answer did you give him?"

She wrote: "I said yes."

To Ellen, the silence that followed seemed endless. She knew how greatly he depended on her, and she feared he would break down into the shame of tears. But he gripped his hands. He was in control again.

"Oh, Ellen!" he said, "Is he a good man? Will he be kind to you?"

Ellen nodded her head to say that he was and he would. Then she wept.

When Ellen left to be married, Erie retired to look after her father. Now in his ninety-seventh year, he had to adjust to another new relationship. His daughter had been his friend and intellectual companion; now she was his doctor and nurse as well.

His world was shrinking fast. He had to give up his walks round the bedrooms, then even the landing was too far, soon he could no longer manage to circle his own room. Movement was restricted to his getting into the chair by the bed twice a day. But his mind reached out far beyond the four walls.

In the winter, he lay looking at the firelight flickering on the oak furniture surrounding him, and once when Erie came in he said "Am I awake? I thought I was in Tŷ Mawr."

In the spring, he would turn his face to the square of the blue sky chequered by frothy branches of wild cherry. It was all he would ever see again of the great outdoors. But he told Erie he was back in the hills of Madras with Katie by his side.

He read extensively, marking in red ink passages that interested him and those which he wanted to discuss with visitors, among whom were newspaper men from the United States, Canada and India, and now, in his mellow years, he treated them with every courtesy.

One day, the new young minister of Pendref came to pay his respects, and Griff's eyes twinkled as he read the tentative, "How are you?" on the pad.

"Enjoying a long sunset," he replied, adding with something of his old self-righteousness: "And if I am not as senile as some men of my age, it is because of my lifelong abstinence from alcohol!"

Ellen brought her first baby to show him. He had always loved what he called "buds", and he crooned over her firstborn in the crook of his arm.

"This is the prettiest baby I have ever nursed." he told her.

Ellen glowed with pride and said she hoped her son would "catch something off him and become a doctor, too." The next year she brought her second son. Griff took him into his arms and pronounced that he was "not quite as pretty as the first one."

For part of each day he wrote letters. He was never diffident about discussing his own death:

I have no fear of what may be in another possible state of being. My duty now is here: take what comes and make the best of it, for self and others . . . If I am asked what I wish for, post-mortem, my reply is, "To meet all my old friends in some kind of purgatory for betterment."

And again:

I sometimes compare myself to one, with others in the ante-room of a Physician, watching for the inner door to open and a call to enter for examination or judgment. I have no fear. My body will be cinerated. I think it not my duty to pry beyond.

His correspondents were all many years junior to him. Not only was his own generation gone, but the generation below him was rapidly dwindling. His views on the next world were crystallised in a letter he wrote to a son of his niece, Gwenddydd, when she died. He quoted the verse from T.H. Huxley's tomb, underlining the last line three times:

And if there be no meeting past the grave,
  If it is darkness, silence, yet 'tis rest.
Be not afraid, ye waiting hearts that weep,
  For God still giveth his beloved sleep,
And if an endless sleep he will — so best.

He enjoyed having Erie sit with him for part of each day. She let him talk without making comment, believing it was harmful to arrest the flow of an old person's thought. He gave her instructions about his funeral. There was to be no service and no fuss. His body was to be removed before dawn to Liverpool crematorium.

One of his regular visitors remarked that the man of science was giving way to the mystic. Yet, although for much of his time Griff seemed to inhabit a sphere remote from this earth, he knew exactly what was going on, and relished all items of news. He was immensely pleased that a letter of his had been shown to the Duchess of York by the King's Veterinary Surgeon at the 1935 International Horse Show, and that she had turned to her daughter, Princess Elizabeth, and said: "This was written by a scientist in his 100th year. Isn't it a simply marvellous piece of penmanship?"

Griff commented to his family that Miss Mair Pugh, his governess, should be given the credit.

Erie recognised that after his hundredth birthday he did not have many more weeks to live. His afflictions were increasing. One was tinnitus, a furious ringing in his ears. Another was the fear that his sight would fail him and that he would be cut off from all communication except touch. And there was the warning given with increasing frequency by his heart that he would not be allowed to die without severe pain.

He resolved to acknowledge as soon as possible the piles of congratulatory messages which had come to him from all over the world. One by one, he methodically answered them all in firm, clear handwriting.

In September, when he had almost finished his task, a letter which gave him great pleasure arrived from the Quartermaster General, India, on behalf of the RAVC there:

> . . . Surra has lost its terror on active service and the progress dates from the day when you found *Trypanosoma evansi* . . .

An earlier post from India had brought a request for a thousand-word article of his reminiscences for the "Indian Veterinary Journal". Griff spent three days writing about his "happy recollections of India, and of the many different kinds of natives I had the delightful pleasure of being friendly with." It was lucid and well written, and as a newspaper piece it is probably unique in having been drafted by a man in his 101st year. He said he had sincere sympathy with the people of India working for their own salvation.

> . . . Of course there have been some lamentable mistakes, such as the feuds between Mohammedans and Hindus, but the law of progress in this world has always been the law of the wheel – construction, destruction, and reconstruction, Vishnu and Shiva alternatively . . .

The editor wrote by return asking for a short message, "an old man's blessing", for the veterinary profession in India which he might publish with the article. Griff's reply was delayed by an accident with puff powder which caused him a week of severe pain in his eyes. By November 11 he managed what was to be the last letter of his life, and his "blessing" was published in the issue of the "Journal" which also carried his obituary.

> I cannot do better than in the prayer of the ancient Welsh bards standing in their mystic, symbolic circle, when opening their proceedings on great national occasions:
> "May God give his Protection
> And in Protection, Strength,

207

And in Strength, Understanding,
And in Understanding, Knowledge,
And in Knowledge, Knowledge of the Right,
And in Knowledge of the Right, the Love of it,
And from Love, the Love of every Being,
And in every Being, the Love of God,
God and every Good."

Now Griff had thanked everybody. His mission was completed and he was ready to let go. But life had one more hurdle for him. In his 101st year he had to deal with a family dispute.

The rift was caused by Katie's will. Fearing lest her son Goronwy's share of the money might be frittered away, she had unwisely directed that the capital be withheld till he reached old age, and that he might use only the interest. Her emotional daughter Towena, always Goronwy's ally, protested loudly. Over the years her resentment had developed into an irrational vendetta against her younger sister Mair, of whom she had always been jealous, and Mair's husband, who was a trustee of the will. She suspected them of having had undue influence over her mother.

Griff knew that Towena's obsession had split his family, but hoped that when they gathered round him on his hundreth birthday they would be united as never before. After the celebration, he anxiously asked Mair if Towena had been "all right". Mair, who could not bear to tell him that her sister had been hostile and had even refused to take her proferred hand, nodded and smiled at him, and Griff sank back with a long sigh of relief. But a few weeks later, Mair's husband, whom Griff had appointed as an executor of his own will many years before, begged to be released from the responsibility. It was no longer possible to protect him from the truth because Towena was making wild accusations and had actually invoked legal aid. Griff sent for his solicitor and appointed an independent executor. He then wrote a postcard which he put in his wallet to be read after his death.

Beware!
It is remarkably common of emotional, sympathetic kind-hearted people *with very limited information* to try rectifying what appears to them a wrong treatment and by interfering

they actually do much greater wrong, injustice, which no one can remedy.

Thus, evil is wrought by *want of thought* as much as by want of heart.

On the other side of the card he printed in Welsh, in capital letters:

ER CÔF AWST
(in memory of August)

This cryptic phrase summed up the bitterness of his realisation that even as they surrounded his bed, his children were still divided, and that the family reunion on his hundreth birthday was a sham.

At the end of November, he became much weaker. "Erie! I am a small boat rocking on a dark sea." Once at twilight, he thought he could just make out the bare branches of the trees against the winter sky. He slept more and talked little, but he liked to have Erie or Mair beside him. In the profound silence of his room, his daughters knew he was living in the past, somewhere in limbo, in an eternity of time and infinity of space. Mair picked up his notebook to express this in verse.

There are no walls; and in that silent place
Lie wide, enchanted spaces, all the grace
Of early boyhood lived through once again.
He walks with long-dead heroes, talks with men.
There is no time; the barriers have worn thin
'Twixt Then and Now, and all can enter in
That love-lit room. How easy it will be
To walk one day into eternity!
And we shall be, when he has gone away
The shadows in the dreams of yesterday.

Towards the beginning of December, his breath came shorter, and he found it a great labour to take his food. He had several heart attacks which left him exhausted. He said he would not try to read anything except Erie's report of the six o'clock news each evening, and essential messages.

"I shall lie quietly and wait for the kind Physician to send for me."

Early on December 7, when the acute distress of the last attack was passing and he appeared restful, he opened his eyes and said to Erie:

"I am very much with your mother now."

He closed his eyes, and died a few minutes later.

INDEX

Aberdovey, 17, 21
Afghan War, 6, 123-4, 145-6, 153, 155, 172
Aldershot, 38-9, 42-4
American Civil War, 1, 6, 50, 68-91, 94
Anthrax, 117, 153, 165, 179
Arthur (Prince), 101

Bangor, 1, 6, 7, 9, 189-94, 197-8, 200
Barmouth, 13, 30, 108, 128
Birmingham, 44-5
Blavatsky, Madame, 178 et seq.
Bombay, 112, 114, 149, 173, 180
Bovell, Dr James, 99
Bridgnorth, 31, 33-4, 36, 95
British Association, 3
British Medical Association, 197
Bruce, David, 160
Brynkynallt, 4, 189-92, 194
Butler, General Benjamin F., 6, 75-7, 80, 84-5

Calcutta, 123-5, 128, 138, 154-5, 161, 165, 180
Cambridge, Duke of, 37-8, 185
Camden Town, 25, 28, 30
Cawnpore, 130-1
Cecil, Lord Adelbert, 96-7
City Point, 80, 82, 84
Cobbett, William, 16, 44
Collins, F.F., 115, 163, 167, 169-70
Collins, J.J., 115, 123
Crimean War, 1, 29, 35
Crocodile HMS, 101
Crookshank, Professor Edgar, 174, 182 et seq.

Cunningham, Dr D.D., 155, 158, 161, 167-70
Curragh Camp, 109, 115, 125, 188-9

Dacres, General Sir Richard, 43
Darby, John Nelson, 96
Dera Ismail Khan, 155-6, 160, 163, 170, 182
Drinkwater, Sir Harry, 183
Drinkwater, John, 85, 196

Eliot, George (Marian Evans), 133-4

Fenians, 42, 49, 101
Filaria evansi, 163
Fleming, George, 101, 170, 181, 184-5
Flint, Dr, 69, 85, 87

George V, 1, 9
Grant, General Ulysses S., 6, 8-9, 71, 85-6, 88, 196-7
Great Eastern, The, 45, 116
Great Exhibition, 29
Grey Nunnery Hospital, 59-60

Henry, Professor Joseph, 69, 72, 89
Hobday, Sir Frederick, 4, 5, 7
Humphreys, General A.A., 81, 84

Ingolls, Brig.-General, 80
Ipswich, 102-3, 106

Jammu, 119 et seq

211

Jones, Professor Sir Henry, 193, 195
Jumna, HMS, 110-11

Kashmir, Maharajah of, 119 et seq, 136
Keshub Chunder Sen, 141-2
King George V, 1, 9
King William IV, 1, 14
Koch, Robert, 30, 56, 117, 169, 172-3, 182

Lacolle, 58-9
Lake Champlain, 58
Lake Michigan, 64
Lake Ontario, 93
Lee, General Robert E, 68, 86, 88-90
Lewis, Dr Timothy, 155, 158, 161-3, 167-71, 182-5
Lincoln, President Abraham, 3, 6, 50, 69, 75, 88-92, 196
Lindsay, General, 68
Lister, Joseph, 183
Liverpool, 44-6, 206
Liverpool School of Tropical Medicine, 117-8, 155, 158, 197
Llanfaircaereinion, 39, 100, 104, 130
Lloyd George, David, 192, 202
Lucknow, 126, 135-6
Lyons, Lord, 69-74, 86-91
Lytton, Lord Bulwer, 98

MacDermid, A.W., 7-9
Machynlleth, 11, 13, 16, 19-20, 23
Madras, 169, 174-5, 178, 184, 205
Martineau, Harriet, 142-4
McGill University, 50-8, 68-9, 93
Meade, General, 69, 80-1, 83-4
Merioneth, 4, 11
Metchnikoff, 117
Meyrick, J.J., 25, 28-9, 32-5, 37, 63, 109, 138, 171-2, 175-7, 188, 200
Milwaukee, 63-4, 66
Minnesota, 63
Montgomerie, Dr R.F., 161, 170, 173, 191

Montgomeryshire, 4, 12, 100, 194, 199
Montreal, 48-50, 56, 58-60, 68-70, 74, 89-90, 92-5, 97-8, 101, 148
Muir, Dr, 68
Mutiny, the Indian, 114, 130-1

New Orleans, 77
Newtown, 32-4
North West Frontier, 6, 14, 152-3
Nowgon, 132-3

Ootacamund, 174-5, 177-8
Osler Library, 57
Osler, Sir William, 99, 169, 197
Oxford, 44

Pankhurst, Mrs, 194
Pasteur, Louis, 106, 117, 158, 173, 182
Patrick, Brig.-General, 85
Petersburg, 79
Phaeton, HMS, 74-5, 88
Phillips, Major, 36-8
Plymouth Brethren, 96-7
Portmadoc, 108-9, 149-50
Potomac, 84, 89
Prince Arthur, 101
Prince Consort, 29
Prince Henry, Duke of Gloucester, 8
Prince of Wales (Edward VII), 119, 185
Prince of Wales (Edward VIII), 7
Pugh, Mair, 14, 18, 206
Pughe, Dr John, 21-3, 52, 94
Punjab, 6, 138, 153-4, 163, 167, 169

Ramsay, General George, 71, 73
Rationalist Press Association, 193
Richmond (Va), 72-79
Royal Artillery, 35, 39, 51, 61, 81, 109
Royal College of Veterinary Surgeons, 4, 30, 197
Royal Veterinary College, 3, 5, 8, 23, 25-8, 32, 51

Saint Lawrence River, 46, 58, 60, 97
Sangor, 132, 134-5
Scott, Capt. Edward, 14
Shillong, 165
Shrewsbury, 11-12, 21, 23, 25, 32
Shropshire, 31 et seq.
Sialkot, 114, 116-8, 122-3
Silchar, 165
Simla, 132, 145-9, 155, 161, 163, 178
Simonds, James, 27
Sioux, 4, 63 et seq.
Smith, Sir Frederick, 170-1, 181, 183
Smithsonian Institute, 69
Spooner, Charles, 23, 25, 27
Steel, J.H., 173-4, 178, 197
Surra, 6, 153-4, 156-63, 167-74, 182-4, 207

Taj Mahal, 115
Tetanus, 106-7
Theosophical Society, 178
Thomas, General, 69, 85-7
Toronto, 93, 95, 99
Towers of Silence, 113
Towyn, 7, 11-12, 14-17, 21, 58, 66-7, 100-2, 109-10, 123, 138, 141-5, 149, 159, 161, 167, 177, 189, 195

Trypanosoma evansi, 158, 160, 170, 174, 207

University of Wales, 189-90, 194, 197, 202

Veterinary Journal, The, 172, 174, 181, 184
Veterinary Record, 6, 161, 170, 173
Victoria and Albert, The, 101
Victoria, Queen, 9, 11, 39, 96-7, 101, 111, 181, 183-5
Virginia, 92

Washington, 6, 68-9, 71, 85, 87-91
Waterloo, Battle of, 1, 13
Wellcome Library, 183
White House, The, 69, 71, 74, 89-90
Wilderness, Battle of the, 68, 70
Wilkinson, John, 35-37, 42, 98, 115
William IV, 1, 14
Woolwich, 35, 37, 43, 102-4, 147-8, 171, 181, 188-90

213